Journey of a Rubber Tapper's Daughter

LUCKY
N U M B E R

Rina Tham

with Lisa Cerasoli

STORY MERCHANT BOOKS
LOS ANGELES
2015

THE STORY MERCHANT

Lucky Number 9

Story Merchant Books
400 S. Burnside Avenue #11B,
Los Angeles, CA 90036

http://www.storymerchantbooks.com

ISBN-13: 978-0-9963689-3-3

Website: www.Lucky Number9.org

Blog: http://luckynumber9-rinatham.blogspot.com

Facebook: Lucky Number 9

Email: Rina@LuckyNumber9.org

Interior Design: Danielle Canfield

Cover: IndieDesignz.com

Tham's lifelong experiences have been expressed so beautifully and intertwined with thought-provoking, practical, spiritual insights. This book will speak to anyone, anywhere in the world. Buddha rightly said, *"Giving help to others is a seed of DHARMA."* So your book will serve as a great motivator for hundreds of years…and beyond.

Baza Guru Rinpoche
Sangaycholing Monastery, Monggar District, Bhutan

Ms. Tham turned a devastating childhood physical trauma into renewed determination believing the universe had something special in store for her. *Lucky Number 9* deserves to be in the hands of young people all over the world.

Kayoko Mitsumatsu
President and Founder, YogaGivesBack.org,
Journalist-producer NHK

LUCKY
N U M B E R

Dear Dr. Homazadeh,

It is my honor to share my journey of a rubber tapper's daughter with you and family.

Thank you very much for your support and opportunity.

Regards,

Kiri

8/23/16.

"Sports changed my life. When I ran, no one stared at my arm. And everyone always cheered louder than I thought they should. My childhood has been blessed. It's perspective, I guess...."

—Rina Tham

First Place, 100-meter dash, 1983

Dedication

To my dearest beloved incredible mom, Thu Ah Nim
To my wonderful mother-in-law, Regina Bernes
To my best friend and husband, Marshall Bernes, MD
And to my family and friends:

You have always supported all my endeavors.
You've been there for every stage of my spiritual development and
we have grown together as a team.
You have given me the greatest gift of unconditional love and
trust.
I am grateful and will treasure you forever and ever.
I love with all my heart & soul.

Acknowledgments

I am so grateful to my worldwide, world-class family—brothers and sisters, relatives, friends, mentors, teachers, gurus, acquaintances, and strangers with whom I have grown and learned from along the way. We've been through good and bad times, happy and sad, and have learned to love freely and without expectation along the way. This has created a genuine bond. Your love and friendship has fashioned me into who I am today. This book would not have been possible without everyone's direct and indirect influences. I'm sending a big *thank you* into the universe for all that you have done!

I am grateful to my great friend, Kayoko Mitsumatsu, for encouraging me to write my journey down.

To my incredible team from Story Merchant Books, thank you. Kenneth Atchity—you believed my story was inspirational and motivational. You told me you could assist in turning my journey on this earth into a beautiful memoir, making one of my dreams a reality. Thank you. *Lucky Number 9* is now a reality.

To Cindy Villarreal and Chi-Li Wong—thank you for your kindness, attention to details, and marketing skills. Let's get this book the exposure it needs to help kids all over the world believe in their dreams.

To my outstanding collaborator and editor, Lisa Cerasoli—I will be forever grateful to you for being my "soul writer," for believing so strongly in my book, and for bringing my inner message out so that I could share it with the world. No matter where I was traveling, from beginning to end, you never failed to Skype, email, or call. We worked so well together. You have been a true professional, so passionate about every detail of this project, and amazing to work with. Thank you.

Thank you Dafeenah Jamaal and Jonathan Mills for the beautiful cover and logo. Thank you Danielle Canfield for the elegant interior design. The book is just as I imagined.

This is my first book. I have shared my deeply personal thoughts about life and love, and little wisdoms I have learned along the way. I care so much for my readers, and I hope you enjoy me sharing my story. I wrote this from memory. There may be tiny inaccuracies in the timeline, and/or details of some events. Thank you for understanding.

My Goal is to Love, Care, and Share

My journey in this moment is to live every day, walking, talking, sharing, caring, and loving everyone. It's vital to my mission with this memoir that I reach young children in schools in both villages and cities around the globe. I want my story to serve as an inspiration to all who read it. I hope you enjoy it, and please pass it along like you would a baton in a 4X100 meter relay—with zest and hope.

I welcome anyone to contact me if they would like to purchase my books in bulk, for schools, or a special group, or their community, whether it's 10, 20, 50, 100, or 1,000 copies. I will make sure that it is available to you at price that is manageable. There are hundreds of thousands of children and people living in underprivileged conditions throughout the world. I want to make sure this story reaches them. My contact information is at the beginning of the book, and you can find me on Facebook: Lucky Number 9.

Present moment only moment.

Rina Tham

The Rubber Tapper's Daughter

chapter one

"DON'T TOUCH IT NOW, Ah Lian. It'll smudge." Debbie scolded sweetly.

I stared at my arm. It was covered in makeup. Debbie had put her facial foundation all over it, and it was drying, I guess.

I had a big day ahead, the biggest of days, and I needed to look my best. This included hiding the scar that started at the shoulder of my left arm and traveled past my elbow, over the wrist, and stopped at my fingertips because there was no place for it to go after that. Looking good for the most important moment of my life included hiding this hideous thing that had trampled into my world some seven years back and taken it over.

Debbie was sister #2. When you have lots of siblings, it helps to number them. Debbie was #2, and Angie was #4. They were in their twenties and both worked for the airlines. At nineteen years old, I was not far behind them age-wise, but they were flight attendants; they saw the world. By comparison, I was quite green.

Both Debbie and Angie were beautiful. At 5'4", with silky black hair and supple, olive skin, they were exactly what a flight attendant should be. They had good work ethic, as did all us siblings, and they were kind too. My sisters were as educated as we could be, given the circumstances. And they were lucky to have been given the good genes. Those were from my mother's side. She has always been "in shape," as they say in America. They chalk that up to a healthy lifestyle and good genes. In Malaysia, there is one basic lifestyle for people of our means: we work. And work. My mother says the rubber trees maintained her "girlish figure."

I look just like my sisters. That means I must be attractive, because they are. Maybe I was once. I remember that like it was a dream—being beautiful. And I remember it like it was yesterday too. Does that make sense? That's the question I've been asking for most of my life: Please help me make sense of it all.…

———•◆•———

There was a long list of things to do every day. This was okay. I have always liked lists.

I was on holiday from school. That meant I was able to go shopping for groceries in the morning, to prepare a nice lunch for my mother and the rest of the family. It was hot and muddy out, but the skies were sunny and a crystal-clear blue. When I arrived back at home, I tended to the laundry first by scrubbing, rinsing, and hanging everything out for the sun to do its magic. After that, it was time for me to light the charcoal and start cooking lunch for Mom. Also, I had to boil water for coffee afterwards.

I enjoyed my tasks, for they made me feel like I was becoming a woman. And I was excited to become a woman and finally fulfill my dreams.

Debbie and Angie had left home to work for the airlines, and, so, preparing dinner was passed down to me. I was ready. I was twelve. It was an honor.

My father owned a phonograph. It was his prized possession. Oh, how I loved it. Music. Whistle while you work. It works! I set my favorite record on the player, and began lighting the stove fire in the kitchen. The *Saturday Night Fever* album blared throughout the bungalow. I recalled how graceful John Travolta looked dancing with his girl in the movie. In my head, John Travolta was dancing alongside me as I stoked the fire. I had a secret crush on him. Okay, maybe it wasn't so secret, as I played this album almost religiously while preparing food. And maybe I wasn't in love with the task of cooking because it made me feel like a young woman. Maybe I just liked John Travolta. Sometimes that happens when you make the best of a situation. After a while, you can't remember what drew you in. You only know that you feel at peace.

Mother eventually came home. She went to work so early every day. By lunchtime, she was often tired. She sat in her chair, massaging a foot, or fixing a shoe. I can't quite remember. Coffee! I had to make her a nice cup of coffee. She called coffee *kopi*. In Malaysia, it was custom to make coffee with a strong black aroma. We used Kluang rail coffee powder that we'd sauté in margarine to bring out the flavor, and then add some salt and sugar. The local coffee shops'

3

main prep areas consisted of metal tanks where the water was kept at boiling temperatures with a tin mug for scooping it out. And the serving cups were always soaked in hot water, so the *kopi* is extra hot. Water is then poured into the sock until it fills up. After it drains into the bottom container, it's emptied into another container and poured back into the sock again so as to catch the finer grains of coffee that seeped through the first time. It's black and strong. We add sugar to make it perfect. Mom calls it "Kopi-O." This aromatic coffee was a genuine treat, and an affordable one. Mother worked hard every day to earn her daily dose.

I boiled water as I cleaned the oily cement floor. That task wasn't as exciting as cooking salted fish with bean sprouts, fried tofu, fried dry prawns with okra, or fried Pak Choi with lots of garlic. There was talent in being a good cook of Chinese cuisine. And cleaning floors didn't make me feel like the young woman I was becoming; it just made my arms tired. But it was on my daily list because the floor accumulated lots of grease from cooking with a charcoal stove. Steam rose from hot dishes and fell heavy onto the floor. All the steam in the world was no match for Malaysian humidity. And the house always reeked of garlic and onion and fried salted fish, which got stinky fast. Fresh starts are important. I was giving the cement floor a fresh start.

"*If I can't have you, I don't want nobody, baby….*" My destiny was not to be a singer. Fortunately, my family did not judge. "*If I can't have you, oh, oh, ohhh….*" I sang like the saying, "like nobody was listening," as I moved about the kitchen on my hands and knees.

4

When you live a simple life, everything has processes. Making coffee had its steps. When pouring the hot water into the sock, the foam at the top must be a creamy caramel brown, not dark. If it's dark, the beans have been over roasted. You didn't strain the coffee back into the sock to sieve it again. Also, there's nothing less right than weak coffee. It's a delicate process. The sock is made of cotton and when it dries up and gets hard, it cannot be used again—just ask Mother, Father, Grandmother, and numbers One, Two, Three, Four, and Five of my siblings—they will tell you. I learned that the hard way.

With the pot securely in my hands, I rushed to the bucket of coffee powder (it was protocol, after all). But this time I slipped on the soapy, oily cement floor.

Mother heard a scream that she later described as unreal and not human.

I guess she made it into the kitchen with a scissors in her hand, but, I don't know.... I don't remember her going into the drawer for them. I just know that she came at me and cut the sleeve right off the dress I was wearing. It was my favorite item of clothing, my lavender and black dress. It didn't actually have sleeves, but it was the area around my shoulder that she cut out as if she had predicted what was going to happen next—in seconds. As soon as the fabric was removed, the skin on my shoulder and arm inflated into a couple of giant bubbles. I was screaming in a very human way now, and crying in agony. The words coming from her mouth were buried by my shrieks. I heard nothing she said. My arm was destroyed. We knew it,

Mother and I. It was revealed when our eyes met as she pulled the sleeve off. We didn't make any more direct eye contact after that. In that second I knew: my dream of becoming a flight attendant and seeing the world was over. The pain in my arm united with the pain that resided where a dream used to live. It happened right there in the kitchen. They embraced like long lost mother and child: my pain and my lost dream. It was horrifying. And I didn't know if the agony I was experiencing was from the boiling water...or not. I couldn't separate the physical pain of the scalding from my heartbreak, even then. It was so intense. I was lost for a moment.

I stared in awe at the magic bubble that was engulfing my arm. My chest felt so heavy that I looked down to see if it had been burned too. My dress was completely dry. Not one drop had landed on any other part of my body. My neck, my chest, my hips, my legs, and my left arm—everything was dry. I was bare footed. My feet were fine. Yet, in my kitchen with Mother frantic, I couldn't shake the pain in my shattered heart. I kept looking around to see if pieces of it were scattered on the floor. I could pick them up, I thought, and put my future back together. I needed to stop all this and go back to just one minute ago when I was dreaming of flying, of meeting John Travolta, of handing him a soft pillow, of him touching my hand and saying, "Thank you, darling."

Maybe I was in shock.

We ran outside and stared at the motorcycle. It was our only mode of transportation. Mother ran off to the closest neighbor's, who happened to be our Uncle John. Thirty minutes later Uncle John pulled up. Mother hopped out, helped me in, and we were at the clinic in a flash. The doctor took one look at my arm and refused to treat the burn. It was too severe. He directed me to the General Hospital.

And then we were at Kluang General Hospital. The waiting room was crowded and busy, as it usually was. Once they saw my arm, I skipped to the front of the line. Ointment was applied in a rush to the bubbles that had engulfed it—to cool down the third-degree burn. We waited on the doctor for pain medication. That came in the form of a shot. Soon after that, I was admitted. Mother stayed for three hours. I felt so bad for her. She eventually left because she hadn't eaten lunch or had her afternoon coffee or a power nap. She had to do housework, wash and cook for dinner, and work the next morning, too.

They took away the magic bubbles (my dead skin) as soon as the painkiller had taken effect. I've chosen never to describe in detail what my arm looked like under it, but imagine an arm without skin….

The twenty-one days to follow consisted of cleaning…and screaming. Every morning a team of nurses came in and scrubbed my arm, the one without the skin. I lived under a mosquito net. Even my bathroom was a bowl next to my bed inside the net. My arm, too, lived under a mosquito net that was put on soft and moist with medicine every night, and then peeled off when it was dry like clay, usually by sunrise.

The other patients at the hospital said they could hear me scream, even when their doors were closed. Everyone knew me. I knew no one.

Mother came when she could, or she'd send siblings with catfish and black bean soup. It was the number one remedy to heal wounds quickly. I ate what I could. Life on a rubber plantation does not stop, so they did the best they could to visit. It didn't matter. I guess a friendly face helped. I don't know.

The staff told me a scary story. There was a girl my age; she even went to my school, though I didn't know her. Anyway, she was burned like me. She didn't do her exercises, though, because it hurt too much to move her arm. Because of this, her arm grew together the way that she held it most, which was bent like she was about to take a sip of soup from a spoon. The skin grew together, and now it's stuck like that.

It hurt so badly to move my arm. It was like reliving the scalding all over again. But I took that tennis ball, gladly, and did my exercises religiously.

It seemed cruel to mother—the type of care I was receiving. She wanted to move me to the hospital in Singapore. I wanted to be anywhere but here. They said she could, but that we'd be responsible for everything if I was moved. That meant if bacteria got into my arm, then it was on us. And I had a constant high fever. It was too risky. With no extra money in her pocket for that type of emergency, Mom decided not to take such a risk. It was out of the question to think further. Also, Dad was not around to help or to take some burden away. *Should she send a telegram to notify Dad?* Telegrams and timeliness did not go hand in hand. Ultimately, she reasoned it would only create worry. From Indonesia, he was too far to be of service. She prayed that things would turn around.

Day twenty-one came. I was sent home. On day twenty-two, I was back at school. Holiday was over. The reception was overwhelming. Sister Dorothy, the Head Mistress, said that everyone had been praying. I just loved Sister Dorothy.

The system for going to school was like a lottery. I had been picked randomly to attend the Catholic school in our area. The Higher Power had been looking over me when I was chosen, and I knew in my heart, as I stepped back onto school grounds, the Higher Power was with me again. Where was He for the last three weeks? I knew not. But I was relieved to feel something other than shattered as I cautiously walked toward my first class.

My inner child's dream was perished. It was taken by the wind like a dry leaf just before a storm. The whole world collapsed on me. I could hardly breathe properly in the beginning. It felt like I was suffocating inside. Still, at school, a sense of peace seemed to dull the pain and slow down the darker thoughts. My future had vanished, but I was okay at the Canossian Convent School.

They had obtained ointment for me. Sister Dorothy saved up for the pink Johnson & Johnson Baby Lotion, and continued to supply me with it through secondary school—for the next five years. She said it would help heal the skin, that it was the best. Sister Dorothy was my first, real mentor. She was responsible for the lotion and taught me to think positive all the time.

When I became blue, which was a lot, I had the chapel. I'd go there and pray, and see other girls there. Sometimes, just from the look in their eyes or a slight nod of their heads, I knew they were praying for me too.

Sister Dorothy, Sister Agnes and the other teachers agreed that I belonged in a special group at school: Prefect. It was an honor to be a part of it. I was one of few chosen based on my grades and my sporty character. My favorite part was that the uniforms had long sleeves. I was safe inside that uniform. I could relax a little. And so I did. By day, I felt the comfort of the convent school. By night, my family welcomed me home as if I was the same. But I wasn't the same. The accident made me very shy. Other than that, I tried to be "me" for them. Because they loved me, I tried my best.

The pain didn't just go away with time. I'd hold it in all day, and then release it after dark. This went on for three years. Nightly, I cried myself to sleep. As much as I prayed to be strong, my heart was chanting a different phrase: *Why me?* I wasn't praying for strength, but answers. *Why me? Why me? Why me?*

By morning, I'd be fine again, for a while. And no one knew. My pillow would be dry. It wasn't until it was time for the laundry that the tracks of my tears became visible: yellow and blotchy all over the pillow covering. As soon as the pillow was clean and dry from the sun, I'd stuff it into the fresh case—hide that pillow again like my arm—and hope that no one noticed how stained it had become from all those salty tears.

And then I'd pray to make it through one more day.

———————◆———————

It looked like Debbie had used half a bottle of foundation to cover my keloid scar. But it looked good. I went to the interview feeling hopeful that maybe I hadn't lost my dream.

It was a success. They liked me and I was to come in a second time.

There were three interviews in the hiring process. This meant I was halfway there. The praying was working. My tears were not in vain. There was hope, and I deserved good things. Debbie and Angie had to have a body check on the third interview. The thought of that was terrifying. I kept telling myself, *you're not there yet, Ah Lian. Live for this interview. Take it a step at a time. And listen to your mother.* She would say, *"Don't cheat. Don't steal. Stand tall. Do more than is asked of you. Live in the moment; it is all you have. And remember to keep your dignity. You can be a janitor. You can be a president. You can be whatever you choose if you live an honest life. Give thanks. Trust. Believe in yourself."*

I had done all that, and so I felt secure.

I didn't get the job with the airline. On the second interview, I mentioned my scar. It was still hidden behind makeup. Debbie had done an amazing job, once again. Maybe she missed her calling....

Anyway, they didn't notice, but I told them. No questions were asked after my admission, and I didn't have to roll up my sleeve. I was grateful for that. But during the interview, after the confession, everything felt different—rehearsed. The smiles, the questions, my answers—it all felt like we were practicing for a play. Our lines had been memorized, and we were reciting them perfectly, but the words no longer held meaning. We were going through the motions. We stuck to the script, and nodded and smiled. But everyone had instantaneously gone from being in the moment, to playing the roles of interviewers and interviewee (including me). It was obvious after I told them about my arm there was nothing left to say. I sat there watching myself like an out-of-body experience. I just wanted to be back home with my family, and, later, my pillow. That's what was going on inside my head. I thought for sure I would collapse when it was over. Play-acting was exhausting.

And then it was over....

I glided from the seat, which was directly across the table from my lost destiny, out the double doors, and into the sun. I was momentarily blinded by its brightness. A strong scent awakened my senses and refocused my vision. I opened my eyes. There, all around me were an abundance of flowers, birds of paradise: Strelitzia. They were thick along edge of the building, framing both it and the pathway up to the double doors. I hadn't noticed them on my way in. Odd. They're my favorite flower. They are so unique, and they smell like the color purple, rich and dense. My pain was gone. Not the physical ache in my left arm. It would be years before that discomfort—a twisting feeling like someone was wringing it out like a wet towel—would fade. The pain that had caged my heart…was gone. Seven years. It took seven years to let go of my dream. You see I didn't have a backup dream. Being a flight attendant was my destiny, and there wasn't a dream to put in its place. It's understandable not to let go.

Part of me thought that I had been strong and gone down fighting. I held onto the vision that I believed to be my future, even after I knew it was gone. *"Don't cheat. Don't steal. Stand tall. Keep your dignity…."* My mother's voice was always there, the voice in my head, guiding me.

Had I? Kept my dignity? Can dignity live alongside delusion? After seven years, I realized; no, it cannot.

I still didn't have a backup plan. I confessed my truth: I had clarity, but I was jumping without a net just like when I bungeed off a small platform into the Victoria's Falls. The free falling was nuts. It felt like suicide. As soon as I hit the water and plunged back up, breathing was so laborious that I thought I was going to die, which caused me to instinctually scream at the top of my lungs. I continued to bounce, spin, and swing under the bridge until I literally ran out of screams. Looking back, letting go of my destiny and grabbing onto faith for the first time felt most synonymous with the bungee jumping into Victoria Falls.

"Okay. I'm ready." I whispered to myself, and to the sun, and to the beauty around me. "Maybe the easy route is not in my cards. I trust you. I know you."

My new dream must be to work hard, just work hard. And see where that takes me. Maybe the easy route is not flying on top of the world and serving beverages with a smile. Maybe it's right here in my backyard. Maybe it's somewhere else. But one thing was for sure; I'll never know unless I let go. I placed one, final request upon my soul: May Thy will and love act upon me.

My eyes closed dry and easy that night. And I let go.

chapter two

AS A LITTLE GIRL in Malaysia, I was so carefree, chasing all sorts of insects and animals: lots and lots of dragonflies, butterflies, mosquitoes, spiders, birds, grasshoppers, bees, dogs, chickens, ducks, and turkeys. In the night, I would chase after fireflies and follow the sound of the crickets or just some loud frogs. They sounded cranky, but in a silly way, and I wanted to catch one. These moments were special and priceless. I was a child, just like everyone else. We were very lucky and happy to have grown up with the jungle animals and insects in our backyard, and to play at the rubber plantation, too. There was an endless variety of colors and shapes and sounds of nature all around like thunder, lightning, heavy rains, strong winds howling—it all decorated my childhood. Bats shrieked. Elephants stomped like thunder. We hardly ever saw them, only broken branches and trees trunks, and their footprints, but that was enough to create a fantastical story for us children to hang onto all week. Orange tigers, honey bears, sun bears, they left their marks on the muddy jungle ground too.

Squirrels, woodpeckers, wild pigs, scorpions, pangolins, and ta-pirs (ant eaters) did their best to stay hidden. They knew father was good with his gun, and they were delicious with garlic in a ginger broth.

Monkeys were not so clever. They were fast, but they liked to swing and play. They were easy for father to capture. Snakes loved to test my family by sneaking into the coop with the chickens. What they didn't know was that we were not picky. Even a snake makes a meal for two.

The eagles would soar in the crystal blue sky, especially after a good rain, which was weekly. Every time I saw an eagle, it felt like God was sending a message that He was close by.

I remember so many colors. The big-leaf mahogany trees were older than Grandmother, some two hundred years or more, and massive, with dark red trunks. Bromeliads were types of trees that didn't need dirt to grow. They wrapped around other trees inside the jungle webs. Their leaves held water and often housed tree frogs and insects, sometimes for their whole lives. We used those leaves to make forts and for umbrellas during rainy seasons. We didn't have Barbie dolls or racecars or any electronics. We found our toys in nature.

Sometimes I played hide and seek with the neighbor kids outside. There were many great hiding spots deep in the rubber plantation. We played nine steps hopscotch. I was an expert at that. Cooking games were one of our things. We would cut the wheat, plants, grass, or hibiscus flowers and cook it up in our magic invisible stoves. One time we were so naughty we stole our neighbor's eggs from their chicken coop and cooked them up. We leapt fast like the jungle frogs into one of our leafy forts just as the he yelled, "Who stole my eggs?" And then we stared into each other's eyes, barely blinking or breathing, until our neighbor gave up and went back indoors. Afterwards, we made a pact to never tell. It has been my lifelong secret. Playing make-believe was common. A wedding took place once. Friends hummed the wedding tune, and we wore my mom and dad's clothes for the ceremony.

We loved to wander to the nearby river and pond to go fishing. Mom and Dad always prohibited it and got angry if they found us wet. A guaranteed punishment from Father was the certain result. He feared we would drown. But we kids loved to fish and swim. (Now you know why most Asians, and especially Chinese people, are not good swimmers....) On occasion, we could catch the fish and prawns with our hands. It was great fun.

The scorpions were most cunning. They'd hide under the latex cups for the rubber trees and squrim out fast.

That's what life in the jungle was like. It was about freedom and survival. We did what we had to do...just like everybody else.

At times, we'd venture far away from home to the rubber plantation to collect rubber seeds. They were round like a marble and so beautiful. We felt proud and special to hold them in our soft hands. I was always counting my tiny treasures. They were my diamonds. We collected thousands. We'd put them in the coop and leave our chickens and ducks to "lay" on them! They'd sleep right on them, protecting our fortune. We had so much joy.

We played in the rain. Being wet from the rain was okay to my father. We were never in trouble from dancing in the rain. It was usually warm and dusty during hot days. At some point, the juice from the heavens would fall onto our faces and skin. It was so refreshing. We were happy and grateful for the gift from the sky. We used it to shower, brush our teeth, and wash all our dirty clothes. The rainwater made it possible for us to mop and clean the floors and windows, and shine up Mom's sedan bicycle too. We'd save it in empty containers, as much as we could, for the next day's use. Water was scarce during the drought season. When that happened, we'd have to load up the sedan bicycle full with baskets of dirty clothes to be washed in the river near our rubber plantation. I can tell you none of us were happy campers when that happened, yet riding the bike with all that laundry created lots of laughter.

Sometimes, there was no water supply. We had to wait for the city to distribute it—about two or three times a week. We had to have all the containers filled up as much as possible to have a reserve for the nine of us and our parents.

Going on long walks, having plays, and getting caught in the rain might have been the best part of our childhood life. I remember as the big and heavy raindrops touched the Earth, the wild frogs, ants, spiders, butterflies, dragonflies, pigeons…all would be running and flying as fast as the speed of light to seek cover. Nothing is fresher than rainwater. The loud thunder was scary, but exciting too. We had a neighbor who was struck and killed by lightning. We were deeply saddened by this, yet it didn't stop us from playing or scrubbing our drain during a storm. It was so great to be outside with no mosquitoes or insects to bite us. The loud thunder had chased away all the animals. Our Rottweiler hid under the bed during storms, howling all night long. But not us. We danced and sang, rejoicing in the pleasures it brought like we owned the world and had beckoned the sky to cry. The wind hit my face clear and cool after a rain. It was happiness with blessings all around.

We would play all day and go home when we saw the nightlight come on at a house near ours. Then we'd rush to finish our chores—homework and housework—before the whole estate turned into darkness. The English management had our generator turn off at curfew, which was 10:00 p.m. That's when our Gotham City went dark and silent. And lullabies, an orchestra of insects, resounded till dawn bringing us peace and harmony and the sweetest of dreams.

———◆———

I was a lucky little girl to be #9 in a series of ten siblings. I had a chance to play when all the others had to work. Jenny was sister #1. Angie, my sister with Cathay-Pacific, was #5, and Debbie, my other sister with Malaysia Air, was #2, as I mentioned. Richard was my #1 brother, but #4 child born of my mother. Pau Chu was sister #6 (but the fifth child birthed from my mother, and #6 in line on the list of siblings after a half sister). They all worked so very hard all their lives.

Each day was more challenging than the one before it, but it was necessary to keep us all clothed and fed.

———————•◆•———————

Mother was twenty-one when she had her first child, Jenny. Eleven years later, there was one after me—the last one, Jason. He's the brother with the soft, tame spirit. He was born in 1966; he was #10. I don't recall seeing him or any of my brothers do much work. It was tradition in Chinese culture: boys don't really work. It was the responsibility of the girls in the family. They helped with the house-work. My sisters, Jenny (until she was sixteen and started running), Debbie, Angie, and Pau Chu were in charge of cleaning windows, collecting and then splitting firewood (so it would fit in the stove). Forget pushups, this kept the girls fit and slim. Daily, they would wash and brush our clothes, then rinse them over and over. This would prepare them for drying, which would happen as they hung under the solar power of the sun.

Ironing school uniforms and chalking the white school shoes for the young ones was a daily task, as was helping with homework.

The rain comes and goes without notice in Malaysia. It's fickle like that. This made the task of laundry extra cumbersome. Clothes that were almost dry would be suddenly wet. Then my sisters would begin the routine of washing and hanging all over again. Sometimes this would happen two or three times in a day. It was frustrating. Occasionally during the rainy season, we'd have to wear our half-dry clothes, or hang our school uniforms and shoes on the stove to dry. Ensuring they didn't catch fire was another job. Mother always needed help in the kitchen—cleaning and chopping leafy Chinese vegetables, long beans, okra, bitter gourd, peeling and pounding garlic and onion, or chilies.

On top of that, not forgetting about the dry clothes the day before was the job of my sisters. Someone had to fold and put them away. (We are talking about clothes for nine children, plus parents.)

There were twelve people eating breakfast, lunch, dinner. We had one bath and one toilet room. The toilet was not on autopilot. We filled it daily with buckets of recycled water from that day's wash. Flushing the toilet was a two-time-per-day event. During the draught season, we did it less. It didn't matter if Mother Nature called, or if there was a stomach emergency. Oh, Diarrhea! It was unfortunate for the whole family when that happened.

After eating, we took turns manually washing and drying the dishes, cleaning tables, and sweeping floors. The house was constantly dirty and in need of cleaning. If you visited our home back then, you were sure to find some sister sweeping, dusting, scrubbing, polishing, wiping, and mostly, doing laundry.

Mother would wake us up with the smell of fresh coffee for our long days. She rose at four in the morning. She was in charge of the coffee normally. That glorious scent would travel to the bedroom and rouse us. It was better than a shouting voice, more gentle. We'd all drink hot coffee from our rice bowl. The bowl that served us rice at dinner became a coffee cup by morning. We could not afford to have both cups and bowls. We'd fill our bellies with coffee and a bit of plain bread—that was breakfast. And then we were off to school. Mother was long gone by then, as she left on bicycle for work by four thirty.

Tham Family

No.	Relations	Names	YOB	Reside
	*Father	Tham Kee Sang	1934	Heaven
	Mother	Thu Ah Nim	1936	Malaysia
1.	Sister Jenny	Tham Ah Moi	1956	Malaysia
2.	Sister Debbie	Tham Sow Keng	1958	USA
3.	Step Sister	Tham Siew Ying	1958	Malaysia
4.	*Brother Richard	Tham Mun Yong	1959	Heaven
5.	Sister Angie	Tham Siew Kin	1960	China
6.	Sister	Tham Pau Chu	1961	Malaysia
7.	Step Sister	Lee Lai Moi	1962	Malaysia
8.	Brother Charles	Tham Boon Hwa	1963	Indonesia
9.	**Myself**	**Tham Siew King**	**1965**	**USA**
10.	Brother Jason	Tham Boon Kieu	1966	Malaysia

* = Deceased In Heaven

I have supplied a cheat sheet to explain the order of children in my family. It was difficult for even us to keep straight. She actually gave birth ten times, but two babies (both girls) did not make it due to jaundice disease. She never talks about those babies, my mother, my woman of steel.

Siew Ying, #3, and Lai Moi, #7, are my stepsisters. My father is their father. Siew Ying moved into our house one hot day in 1968. She came from her family's plantation, Lambak Estate 2. It was four miles one way. She just showed up. She didn't even have a bag, but she moved in for good. Nothing was said about it. I later heard from Siew Ying that the siblings bullied her badly. They wanted her out. We were at capacity. Who could blame them? Another person meant more of everything—clothes to clean, food to cook. And she took up space, like people do. We didn't have much of that in our two-bedroom, 800-square-foot home. She was one more person who fought for the window in the bedroom every night. We slept all in a row, like Dominoes. The first one in the room claimed the place right by the window. It was always a race for that coveted spot. Now there was another body in the game, another Domino in the row. With the addition of my first stepsister, we were now nine deep. But Siew Ying's decision was made. After a while, Dad put a stop to us chasing her out. We all lived under the same roof, he said. After that we went about our business and didn't complain about the space.

Her younger sister, Lai Moi, #7, never did live with us. She was two years older than I was. She was given to the Lee family. They were rubber tappers, too. No one really saw her. I didn't know much about Lai Moi growing up because of that. Years, and then decades, faded into the past without knowing Lai Moi. Now, we are connected with three of her kids like distant relatives. We meet up for dinner annually to catch up, especially on the Chinese New Year.

There must have been a "Vacancy" sign on our door the summer of '68, because Pau Chu, sister #6, showed up one day also. She came on foot, too.

Pau Chu has become my beautiful soul sister. She was given away immediately after a breech birth because she almost took my mother's life. Ironically, that incident happened at home when Grandmother was the midwife. Mom nearly bled to death. She was sent to the emergency room at Kluang General Hospital. Dad had to donate his blood to revive her. Pau Chu was then given away to a Hakka neighbor. The man was a bus driver. His wife was a rubber tapper.

Pau Chu was ill treated by this new family. She lived most her young life in captivity. She was free to work, but then afterwards they chained her to the kitchen table. She was fed scraps. One day she ran. That's the day she joined us. She was in bad condition—under nourished, skinny, shy, without any sense of self or confidence.

She was free at our home, but always wanted to hide under the table. That's where we'd find her. We'd let her stay there for we knew not what to do. She was not educated at all. Mother had her continue with daily work, which was all Pau Chu knew. She worked in the rubber plantation, worked in the field with construction labor workers, and in the coffee shops, too. She carried heavy blocks of cement, and worked a lot around the house. She was the hardest worker anyone had ever seen.

Pau Chu's life has been unfortunate and challenging. Her husband, who was a chef, passed away when he was only thirty-nine years old. He went to a regular check-up in a Singapore Hospital, and died of a heart attack right there in the examining room. He left her behind with their beloved one-year-old son, Edward. Pau Chu was devastated to raise Edward as a single parent. Even today the shock of this event has stayed with her. Should we call it fate? Destiny? What? Some things I will never understand....

It took a long time for Pau Chu to mix and be normal. Relatives, neighbors, and especially strangers were a threat to her—anyone who didn't live in our house. She was terrified all the time. I'm sure we bullied her, too (especially Mom, she just disliked her). I think Mom blamed her for the breech birth, for Grandmother being the midwife that day, and for nearly dying. Grandmother talked Mother into giving her away. My guess is that Mother didn't so much dislike her, but I bet Pau Chu's presence drudged up a feeling of guilt from having given her up at birth. I'd watch Mother keep her head down and her eyes averted when she was around Pau Chu.

In spite of all the ups and downs and the roller coaster of her very tough life, she stuck around. Pau Chu held on and never gave up. And her heart has remained kind. Her heart only knows how to give. She is the caregiver to our eighty-year-old mother today. She loves, cares, and shares her life in the best way she can. In my eyes, Pau Chu is my nightingale.

I think Pau Chu must have possessed an extra amount of faith to choose to leave her original home. To understand that it's our responsibility to change our own circumstances is one thing, but to act on it takes courage. I mean, she was six. She didn't even know us. She knew no other life. I guess she was born with double the courage.

Mother always said, "Pau Chu was not satisfied with her life, and so she made a change. She has determination, that girl."

25

"What's determination?" I asked. I was only three, and didn't know all the big words yet. "Is that what it means to walk five miles all by yourself when you're just a little girl? Is that like knowing your directions, Mama?" Pau Chu had never been to our house. How did she know the way?

"I would say, Ah Lian, that knowing your way without having a map is exactly what determination means, my love."

Pau Chu was older than I was by four years. I was blessed to have another sibling show up on my doorstep and become a very important part of my life, especially one with the determination of Pau Chu.

chapter three

MY FATHER AND MOTHER met only once before they were formally married. It was a setup, an arranged marriage. A matchmaker put them together. It was often like that in Malaysia in the Chinese culture. It was also common for Muslim and Indians, too. Much importance was placed on marrying within your culture. Mother was strongly against mixed marriages, which could happen here, as we all seemed to resemble each other and live so closely together. Later, when Mother had children of her own, she proved the strength of her belief in this philosophy. She worked double shifts in order to save enough money to move twenty miles further out of town into a Chinese community to prevent us kids from interacting with Indians and Muslims, for fear we would fall in love. She gave up complimentary housing from the English management on the rubber plantation, sacrificed sleep, and gave up free time with family to keep us divided.

It was also Chinese custom that both the woman and man agree to the match in order for the union to occur. That was a good thing, I guess. Both parties have the opportunity for input. But there was a limited amount of time (one or two meetings) to determine if you wanted to spend your life with a person that was picked out for you by a matchmaker—a total stranger. How does a woman meet a man one day and decide to spend the rest of her life with him the next? Truly knowing a man, his heart and his soul, in one day could not be possible. Could it? It must have been more about compatibility.

My father was a tall, dark, handsome, talented mechanic and had "eyes for his work"—he was very focused and hard working. He could fix all sorts of foreign Japanese and English cars, tractors, bulldozers, machineries, etc. He was gifted with languages, too. He was bilingual—spoke Tamil (with Indian and Muslim accents), and many other Chinese dialects fluently. He was very friendly and nice to the neighbors, but he was hot-tempered around the house. It was hard to tell if he had any respect for the women he loved, or if that respect stopped at his mother. He was too friendly at times, too, which is how I came to have two stepsisters.

My mother was an angel. I have often referred to her as the Angel: Goddess of Mercy. She even looked like an angel, even at nineteen. She was a dark-haired beauty. And the Universe gifted her these beautiful cheekbones that made her face always look like she was about to break into a smile. There was a peace about her; welcoming energy radiated from her heart and soul.

And so it was determined that they were a match: Mother's compassion would complement Father's temper. They agreed to be married.

Mother stated that she believed Father would work hard, and could fix things. He had skills, and that was important. No one knew what the future held, but she didn't want hunger to be another worry. If she married a skilled man, he would provide. There would always be food for their future family.

Even though my mother is my angel on Earth, I often wonder if my father's handsome face weighed in heavier than it should have in her decision-making back then.

They were at each other's throats throughout my childhood. They had made enough babies that—to the outside world—it looked as if they got along quite well. We never saw it.

When Father came home early from work—between three and four on the rainy days—Grandmother, who was in charge of us, would cause trouble by telling tales. She devised crazy stories about our alleged criminal behavior. He would beat us with a hanger, or a belt, or a *rattan* (cane).

Grandmother always had a story. She was mean. We lived with her in Mengkibol, Kluang when the family was just starting. This is before we lived in the Englishmen's complimentary housing to save money for our first home—the 1,200 square foot four-bedroom house at Lucky Garden, which was also in Kluang.

She was my father's mother. Grandmother adored her son, and her first grandson, Richard (brother #1). She worshipped him, too. He was her blue-eyed boy, and the epitome of perfection in Grandmother's eyes. But even though Richard was brother #1, he was not the first-born child. That was Jenny, in 1955. That was a problem.

Grandmother hated girls. She said that girls were deficient, good for nothing, should be tossed away. It angered her intensely to see

Mother give birth to Jenny. Her bitter words were like giant metal clutches holding my father captive. "If your wife cannot give you a son, maybe you married the wrong woman. It's not right. It's not fair. A man deserves sons!"

It wasn't long before Grandmother convinced Father that if his wife "cannot produce sons," he should, literally, try with another woman. This is how the affair with my mother's sister began. Aunt Ah Lan was seeking help from Dad to learned how to drive a car. With the blessing from my grandmother, he began his affair with Aunt Ah Lan. In June of 1958, much to Grandmother's dismay, my mother gave birth to a second child, Debbie. But there was hope. Mother's sister, Aunt Ah Lan, was due just five weeks later. She gave birth right on time to a healthy baby girl. And that is how Siew Ying came to be my first stepsister.

When Grandmother wasn't telling tales and praying for meteorites to fall from the sky and land on the young female members of the Tham family, she was a famous spiritual healer in the Mengkibol Village. She specialized in healing children, especially babies. People came from all over Malaysia to have Grandmother place her hands on their sick kids, and say her special prayers. Then the children would ingest her patented homegrown herbal organic medication and be healed. She was very good at her job. Because she was in such high demand, she rarely left the house. She never knew who would show up in need of her magical powers of healing. Once we moved to Lambak Estate 1, which was five miles away, it was up to us to visit Grandmother if we wanted to see her. I went to visit, she was my grandmother, but when she laid her hands on me when I had a fever, I never once felt those magic powers.

Eventually, Father got a job logging. This meant he had to work far away. He went abroad to the foreign land of Indonesia.

After that, we only saw him once a year during the Chinese New Year. Life became different. We all pitched in even more to help Mother. It was hard without Dad, at first. And then it became easier and easier as time went by.

Mother was left to be in charge of the family. Because she practiced Buddhism, she ruled with a kind heart. She strongly believed her kids should learn Chinese and should not branch out and go to English schools. (Father ended up trumping her beliefs, ultimately.) She played both roles of mother and father in a very positive way for her children. Mom worked in the rubber plantation in the early morning, and raised pigs in the evening. She never failed to pray and worship with joss sticks, and she had a kerosene lamp lit twenty-four hours daily (as that was cheaper than oil) to honor the Almighty. It was compulsory for her. She gave thanks to the sky, Earth god, and ancestors before eating her breakfast, lunch, and dinner. This was how she paid respect to the Almighty Power within her that empowered her with the ability to love, share, and care, and be a strong provider for her big family.

She was a strong-willed mother with a plan: she wanted a better life for her children and her family. She received $800 to $1,200 ringgit per month from tapping trees. Those were her wages if she could tap 500 to 1,000 trees a day.

To pull that feat off regularly, she had to rise very early…and she needed help. Without it, she would have never earned the extra money to purchase her dream house, and she was determined to eventually move away from the rubber estate plantation, and far away from Grandmother, where we all lived in complimentary housing from the English management: rubber plantation's Estate 1 housing.

One morning, Mom started waking me up to go to work with her. I was finally old enough to chip in for our survival. In the beginning, I was very reluctant to wake up. But once I shook the sleep from my limbs, and put a bit of bread and coffee in my belly, I appreciated and enjoyed every minute with Mom, even the dark solitude of the bicycle ride.

I would sit on the back of the bike, breathing in crisp air that was bordering on frigid. The tropical early morning breeze was laced with the aroma of coffee and tasted of charcoal from the neighbor's cooking.

Holding on for dear life behind my mother on the bicycle was top priority. I wrapped my arms firmly around her tiny waist and off we went. That was how we got to work. I held on so hard some days, I thought I'd squeeze her spirit right out through her ears. But she never complained. This helped steady the ride, but also kept me warm (her body heat). I'd pray as we rode—that we'd go to and from work safely on the bike together. That was my mantra. I lived in the moment when I was on holding onto Mom and sailing through the streets at dawn. At the same time, Mom's old sedan metal bicycle was very strong and steady. It was able to carry two to three people, two big empty containers for the latex, a special tapper knife, Mom's favorite bamboo yoke (of vital importance), two big buckets, two small buckets for Mom and me to collect latex, our lunch, coffee, and some dry latex, which were the "winnings" from the daily rubber tree tapping. Sometimes, we would pick up firewood and pack that onto the metal bicycle. It was heavy duty. Still, I prayed. Maybe I was more afraid of the dark jungle than I was of that bike, cause it never failed us.

There was no light on the way to our rubber plantation. The sun had not risen. The streets were not lined with special lights and wires connecting them like in America. But these memories of being alone with Mother, holding her tightly with my eyes closed, feeling the brisk air lap at my face, this fed my soul.

Roosters crowed like clockwork.

When we arrived at work, it was still total darkness. The Quran (Muslim prayers) would blast from loud speakers to the early shift workers and to the monkey, birds, bats, wild boars, snakes, scorpions—preparing us all for the day ahead.

Sometimes we were assigned to the far away plantation. (Daily, it was a random assignment. If we were lucky, we got the nearest rubber plantation. If we were not lucky, we were given the faraway rubber plantation.) The faraway rubber plantation was two to five additional miles on bicycle. The road was dusty, uneven, rough, and the rain came and went. On days when the rain was thick and steady, we'd return home, which resulted in the loss of one day of income. We could not often afford to do this.

So most days, when we got unlucky, we'd arrive at the faraway plantation soaking wet. It was cold, yet we'd work through it. After a couple of hours, we'd always be dried by the grace of the sun.

Mom would smoke her first cigarette at the onset of tapping. It was ritual. This created lots of smelly smoke in the dark. This was to let the other tappers know that a "man" was working beside them. This was her "Beware of Dog" sign. The price of cigarettes was worth it to her. She was never hassled by the other male tappers. Men left men alone on the plantation. Her second cigarette was to be smoked after lunch break. This prevented both the men from bullying *and* the mosquitoes from biting. Of course, I was young. This is what I was told. For all I know knew, maybe she was stressed out. Maybe it was because father was gone and she was in charge. Maybe nine mouths to feed led her to smoking two cigarettes per day, just to get through it all. Maybe it was her one guilty pleasure, and nothing more than that. Even Mother must have desired some things, like other humans. I would imagine so, anyway.

In general, lunch break was around ten to twenty minutes long. This time was better spent collecting firewood for the evening. It was usually windy. We'd have to collect the latex quickly before it dried up; the breeze could do that. Then we'd collect the firewood and use the remaining five to ten minutes to eat. We'd have leftover food and cold coffee. That would be gobbled up hastily, and then we'd resume the task of getting our buckets ready to collect the latex, the produce of our day.

When Mom really needed the money, she'd request to do double shifts (two plantations in a day). On those days, Mom and I would tap 500 to 600 hundred rubber trees at 4:00 or 5:00 a.m., then Jenny and Debbie, Pau Chu, or another girl, would clear it all out for us and bicycle it back to the plantation station. They'd meet us there where Mom would explain the process of weighing, and then rush to the next plantation to tap another 500 trees at 11:00 a.m.

She'd try to finish all the work by herself, but with our assistance, it was more manageable.

Again, after the second set of trees were tapped, we'd all meet at the plantation station to weigh the produce we'd accumulated. A total of 1,000 hundred trees were tapped on those days. My sisters worked in full force at both plantations. This was on the days we didn't have school, like holidays, weekends, and summertime. I found it to be fun and exhilarating. I relished in the togetherness of it all. It wouldn't have been possible without hard work and teamwork.

My eldest sisters found this scenario to be stressful. They worked the plantations for years like this with Mother. I only did it once in a while, so for me, it was a real rush.

chapter four

ON APRIL 15, 1770 in England, a clergyman and chemist by the name of Dr. Joseph Priestley noticed that a piece of material from an Indian gum tree was extremely effective at rubbing a pencil mark clean from a piece of paper. The term, "rubber" originated upon his discovery.

—————•◆•—————

In the late 1800s, a roadshow scientist named Henry Ridley, who had discovered many new species of flowers and plants in Malaya, convinced British and Chinese planters to grow rubber when no one was keen on it. (Malaya was the name for pre-independent Malaysia, before 1958.) Coffee was the big thing then, so it took some skill to talk the British Colonial Government into seeing the commercial potential in rubber tree planting.

By 1897, there were 140 hectares of rubber trees throughout Malaya. (One hectare is equal to 100 acres.) A few years later, halfway across the world in the United States of America, cars were being invented. This brought on a new need for tires, rubber tires. By 1913, there were 322,000 hectares of trees in Malaya. Now, there are over 1.3 million hectares of rubber tree plants in Malaysia. Rubber tree tapping is considered one of the greatest achievements in Western colonial enterprise.

———◆———

In 1915 Kluang was founded. It was named after the Malay word, *keluang*, which meant flying fox. These fruit bats flourished until hunting and the rubber plant industry slowly took over abolishing their natural habitat little by little. Today, they are virtually extinct.

———◆———

The American man hopped out of the van, gazed in wonder at the towering forest of rubber tree plants. "What is that stink? It's rank. What is that?" he said, fanning the acrid, unpleasant odor away from his face.

"That stink is the smell of money, my friend." The Malaysian man behind the wheel of the van answered with a wry smile.

———◆———

It's no easy thing to tap a rubber tree. It's very labor-intensive. Tapping is a tedious process. My mother sharpened her knife religiously after a power nap every day (or early evening) after work for thirty minutes so it could cut into the trees the next morning. An unsharpened knife would permanently damage a rubber tree. There were professionals who sharpened knives all day for the tappers; it was their only job. My mother could not afford that, so she did it herself.

After she dressed in her tapping clothes, which consisted of a long-sleeved shirt, a headscarf called a hijab (which covers the head and shoulders but leaves the face open), and long pants, mainly to keep away sun and mosquitoes, she got her headlamp ready. Tappers wore carbide helmets—headlamps that were filled with carbide because kerosene and batteries were too pricey. That was a tricky process, too, getting the headlamp ready. Checking to make sure the line was clear for gas to pass through and that the right amount of water was being dispensed was a priority to ensure that the lamp wouldn't explode. They were also extremely hot to the touch. The carbide smelled really bad, like a rotten egg.

Between the bark and wood of a rubber tree there's a thin layer called the cambium. Accidentally cutting into that thin layer would kill the tree—thus the need for a sharp knife, and steady hand. The cambium is responsible for growth; it produces bark and wood. The tree will be ruined, you see, if you cut the cambium.

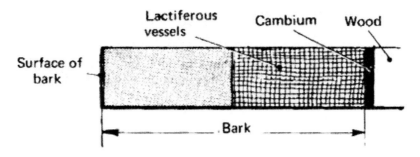

It was essential to come within 1.5 millimeters of the cambium to get the milky latex liquid to flow from the tubes—the lactiferous vessels—that reside directly in front of the cambium. When trees matured to the age of five (50 centimeters in circumference and 1 meter high) they were big enough to be tapped.

A metal ribbon that is secured to a wood lath is wrapped about the tree, 1.1 meters high and at a 30° angle. With an awl (the knife-like tool), a tapper cuts along the edge of the wrapped metal ribbon until the initial cut and the end cut are in the same vertical line.

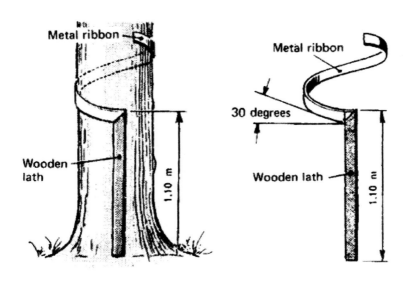

A gouge instrument must then move/push the bark aside by digging into the tree a bit. This is where the tapper needs to pay special attention, too. The bark is 6 millimeters total. The depth of the opening made by the gouge must be 4.5 millimeters exactly.

Then a gutter is added to the bottom channel. A latex cup is then tied to the tree below the gutter to catch the milk...and that is tapping a rubber tree. The latex flows along the cut, down the gutter, and into the cup. The latex looks like a cross between whole milk and Elmer's glue. Harvesting the latex at the right time is crucial. A good harvest produces 236 milliliters (1 cup) in about three hours.

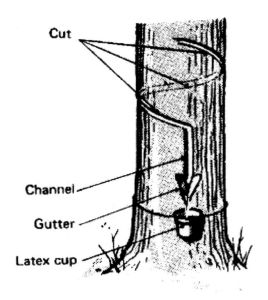

The latex from the first harvest is not good for several days. Still the bark must be cut (the wound must be reopened) and the milk must be drained to make way for the good latex. Four hours after the first harvest, it's time to clean the cup. Two days after that, the tapper returns to collect the next cup of latex. Then the next release of latex is considered to be *the good stuff*. This is a general overview of the process.

Collection centers are all around the estates. Cylinders and empty drums that contain Ammonia gas—to preserve the latex and prevent coagulation—are scattered about. Farmers bring the latex to the centers for measurement (weighing). This is after a dry sample is taken to determine the "dry rubber content" of the collection, then the latex is measured, filtered, and poured into the drum. When enough liquid latex is collected from a center, it's transported by car to the main area, the Society Center, and it goes on from there.

My mother did this twice a day: she carried 50 to 80 kilograms of latex in a yoke across her shoulders to the centers for weighing. She was quite lucky to have a bicycle; many had to walk, sometimes five miles, to get their collection weighed. The rich tappers had it very good. They owned motorized bikes. Their trips to and from the center were nice and short. But that's a lot to carry over a period of time. Fifty kilograms is over one hundred pounds.

Tapping at daybreak is essential, to ensure a maximum amount of latex. One third less latex is produced if the tree is tapped too late in the day. Four to five hundred trees are generally divided into two

41

groups, and then tapped on alternating days. They produce the most latex this way. Slowly, the tapping moves up the length of the tree. This takes about seven years. Then tapping at the ground level can begin again. A tree can endure this process three times, or for twenty-eight to thirty years. After that, the latex production is too low to be worth the trouble. Originally, it was custom to burn the tree down, on the spot, and plant a new one when it was of age. Nowadays, rubber wood (from the Hevea brasiliensis, or the Parà rubber tree) is used for furniture, flooring, other construction, and even to make toys. It's beautiful and sturdy wood.

Rubber trees grow 23 meters high, 1 meter around, and cover 36 million acres of earth in Asia, Africa, and Tropical America. Ninety rubber trees comprise an acre, meaning there are roughly three billion rubber trees living on our planet today.

Like my grandmother on my father's side, my mother's mother also believed that girls were good for nothing. Mother never received a formal education because of this; she just tapped trees, constantly taking good care of the family and household.

Starting when she was five, she learned how to raise nice pigs. She raised them to be fat and heavy, so she could sell them by weight to gain more profit. When she turned eight years old, she was finally of age to tap up to 500 trees a day with her mother. She assisted until she was old enough to do it alone, around the age of eleven or twelve.

When she became a mother, at twenty-one, she tapped 600 to 1,000 trees a day. There were mouths to feed.

She tapped until she was almost sixty.

In her lifetime, my mother has tapped rubber trees more than five million times. This means that she has been singly responsible for contributing enough latex to produce half a million tires world-wide.

By 1974, after thirty years of tapping, she had saved enough money to purchase her 1,200-square-foot dream home at Lucky Garden Estate in Kluang. It wasn't until years later, when Dad earned extra money, that he bought a 2,300-square-foot, single corner house for the family at Taman Indah Jaya. That was in Kluang as well.

This place is just two miles away from Lucky Garden, her first family home. This is where she feels most comfortable. Mother resides there to this day with Pau Chu looking after her. No matter where Mom has traveled, she has always insisted on returning to this place—the place she calls "Home Sweet Home."

chapter five

I BELIEVE IT WASN'T my mom's strong muscles, but Buddhism that gave her the ability to tap trees day after day for half a century.

With Malaysia being a country comprised of Chinese, Indian, and Muslim people, there is religion wherever you go. If you didn't agree with one faith, just walk next door to the neighbors and pray on your knees to Allah. If that wasn't your thing, the Hindu family down the path would have you in for sunrise worship. If you came upon a friendly grasshopper along the way, be sure to bring him...he might have been someone special once. If that didn't feel right to your soul, there would be a Mass at school on Monday—the Catholic school where I went. So, I grew up in a four-faith community, really, but the most impactful was Buddhism.

Mother honored Buddha twice per day outwardly, but she lived by His Law 24/7. On the first and fifteenth of every month of the Chinese calendar, we prayed a little extra. She also worshipped the sky and Earth gods, and other ancestors, too. On those special occasions, Jenny and/or Pau Chu had to slaughter a chicken or duck or turkey, and bring along some roasted pig to make offerings. We also had to fold special papers with gold and silver leaves (representing money) into triangular shapes and stack them up together like little gold bars. The aroma of jasmine filled our space of worship and sacrifice—joy sticks were used for offerings. At the end of the prayers, we waited about twenty minutes, then burned the money; this was how we mailed it to God for our forefathers. And the chicken or pig or whatever edible had been sacrificed was brought into the kitchen for cleaning and cooking. Dinner would be blessed that evening.

The first and the fifteenth on the Chinese calendars were the days of the full moon. Temple held a big festival and prayer ceremonies. They would have a path of hot coals ready. All who wanted to cleanse their souls of negative energy could walk on them. They were also used to ward off bad luck. This was an occasional practice in nearby temples. Nowadays they call it fire walking. People generally pay a fee to be trained to do it right.

We went to Tomb Sweeping Day annually as well: Ching Ming. To honor our dead ancestors, we'd bring food, tea, and alcohol and sweep their gravesites. This usually happened during the vernal equinox (spring). I guess you could call it spring-cleaning.

This I remember very well: Once in a while, before the original date of Ching Ming (April third or fourth annually), we'd pray and invite our ancestors (in spirit) back into our physical world. This is channeling. We'd channel them and ask how they were doing. We'd ask about their desires and needs. Then we'd scribble their names on paper, and burn it. Then we'd mail the ashes over to them in the spirit world, like we did with the money in the Buddhist worshipping. This would ensure that whatever they desired—a house, a mate, a car, a dog—they would come to them shortly. Then we called upon our dead relatives, and they came down. It was like touching the greatest truth. It was scary. Intense. Heavy. Uplifting. All these spirits would float in and out of bodies and speak to us. It was magical. We channeled my grandfather and my grandmother successfully that day. Grandfather asked for a sweater, a blanket, and a house; I heard him speak this request. We made tiny furniture out of paper, then burned them, and popped the ashes in the mail promptly.

That was my first heavy-duty experience with the power of religion. It would be years before I was to develop a true understanding of that event. And it would be decades before I'd be able to worship regularly and live with the kind of faith Mother seemed to possess so naturally.

Summer of 1983

It was my time to go into the world and see what plan it had for me. I was nineteen. I had graduated.

Angie had made a vow to never be a rubber tapper. She was with the airlines. Even though it was Angie's vow, I secretly took it into my heart, too. I didn't want to tap trees for my whole life either. Debbie was married and living in the capital of Malaysia. That's where I wanted to go—to the "University of Life," which I believed was in our country's capital: Kuala Lumpur. Mother gave me permission. She said, "Be a bother to no one. Work for your food and your shelter. Leave Debbie and her pilot husband to live their lives. You may go, Ah Lian."

I wasn't smart like my older sisters. I wasn't a stupid girl, but studying my school subjects never came easy to me like it did them. By the time I was in secondary school, it was clear that I was going to "just get by." I burned the midnight oil studying regularly—history, sciences, English, mathematics. Friends would come over to quiz me. Sisters would help, Angie and Jenny, and not understand why I took so long to memorize so little. I would put in one hundred percent effort to receive a fifty percent on a quiz. I wasn't cut out for the academics of school. I was cut out for sports, though.

We had quite the track team. We were number one in the state all the years I was on it. I was always positioned as first or last leg of the relay team. I liked that kind of pressure. It fed my soul and my drive. My positioning would depend on the team we were competing against. And while the last leg was my favorite spot, it gave me the biggest butterflies, too.

When I wasn't in track working on my 100M speed-of-light dash, or my relay skills for the 4x100M, or with the javelin, or shot put, or long jump, I was busy practicing badminton in the indoor and outdoor volleyball courts. The lottery at my school didn't result in just a few fortunate girls getting a good education. It resulted in sports teams that went to state every year—and won. Apparently, the school got lucky, too, with this system. This happened with badminton and volleyball as well. We went to state, and we always won.

Due partly to my athletic abilities, people were excited to see me every day at school. I was shy before that because of my arm, but sports changed everything. I wasn't the best student, but I was nice, and had a severe amount of self-control built into my bones. They made me school monitor and prefect for these reasons: I was kind and well disciplined. "It's a good combination for a leader," I could hear Mother saying as I watched over my classrooms with care.

I was captain of the Red House. That meant I was the person in charge of a group of sports teams. I won more trophies and medals than I have ever been able to keep track of during my secondary school years at Canossian Convent School.

Charles and Jason, my brothers, saw me compete a couple times. That felt special—to have some family see me do something that came so natural to me. Our school had to compete at their school, and so Charles and Jason and their friends were all there. It was thrilling to see the surprise on their faces. To hear them cheer for me was the greatest thrill of all.

I'd bring home my acheivements and say, "Mom, here's another gold medal." And she'd say, "Oh, great," then turn her eyes back to her work. That was enough though. I know Mother would have liked to see her little girl fly like the wind over the finish line, but she had to tap trees. She saw me run free in her heart; at least that's how I felt when she looked at me. Later, we'd joke about not having to worry about having a wedding present to give to my future husband, because whoever got to marry me would be handed all my medals as my dowry. Mom had obviously done more than glance at them if she thought they'd suffice as a dowry.

Dad saw so many medals piled on the floor when he came back from Indonesia for the Chinese New Year one holiday, he spent his free time constructing a shelf to hold and display them in our living room. They looked like masterpieces, real art, right on the wall in the center of the main living area. I was Picasso. My medals, although just a brassy gold, added vibrancy and energy to our household, and stimulated conversation. I was so proud.

I recently found a big straw basket of them. They were broken and faded, gold and silver in color, but packed up carefully nonetheless. I found them by Mom's storage room. This confirmed she really did save them as a dowry for my husband. I brought them home to the USA. Someday, I plan to restore them, find a new home for my treasures that hold so much sentimental value. I remember holding each one so tight after every race. That basket of memories was a wonderful discovery.

When I was ready for the real world, Mom said, "You're tough, you're nice, you listen well, and you know about teamwork. You will do well out there. Go, be the leader that you are, Ah Lian."

Sports taught me a lot about teamwork. Even when I felt nervous about not getting straight As, I was secure in knowing that as a member of a team, I could shine. I was not the type to ever let teammates down—not my mother, sisters (or brothers) at the rubber plantation, and not my track, badminton, and volleyball teammates.

I had saved all my Chinese New Year's gifts—the red packets of money since I was a toddler—from aunts, uncles, and every other relative. But when I counted it up at nineteen, it didn't add up to much.

Richard (brother #1 and child #4), Grandmother's blue-eyed boy, and the first one to carry the last name of Tham, was the one member of the family who was able to attend college. The family had saved enough for one child out of ten, and it went to the #1 son: Richard. I didn't so much mind, as studying didn't come natural to me, but Angie was furious. Jenny, who was the actual first-born child, had more serious issues at the time, so school was not top priority for her. But both Debbie and Angie were exceptionally intelligent and cut out for studying. That mattered not in our culture. And so, the blue-eyed boy of Grandmother's eye went to Tunku Abdul Rahman College in Kuala Lumpur, where he studied business right up until he fell head over heels for a girl one town over from Kluang. He was one semester shy of graduating when he dropped out of college. By that point, three and a half years worth of tuition had already been paid. Nine other children, who were all interested in higher education, were left with no college money. Richard upset the family deeply with his decision to be married prior to graduating. He begged for wedding funds, and finally borrowed the money from his best high school friend, Teng Fook, from Australia. In the end, Dad contributed, too, as it was clear Richard was determined to marry. "This is what love can do to a man. Poke out his eyes so he can't see straight!" …You know who went on (and on) like that about the whole incident.

Angie cried and cried when she heard the news. He took all the college funds…and in the end there was no degree to show for it. Angie was so smart. That's when the family discovered that the only thing bigger than Angie's brain was her temper. She and Richard nearly got physical over it. The whole family had to step in. It was tough times. I felt for everyone. I loved them both. I didn't understand the depths of romantic love back then to know why Richard would do what he did…but I definitely had a deep understanding of what freedom meant, and how long and strong a person can hold onto a dream, for I still had mine. Angie felt like Richard was given a dream, took it for granted, and because love is blind (and deaf and dumb and selfish), he destroyed it. Maybe to Richard, college wasn't always in his heart. What was a dream come true for Angie, could have been a burden or a curse for Richard. People are different. We may never know….

This is what led Angie to Cathay Pacific. With no hope of a formal education, she needed a job. She wanted something that would teach her about life, and help her to see the world, and something that would pay well, too. A stewardess suited her needs better than anything else that seemed possible at the time. She's one of the strongest women I have ever known. She made a good living for herself at Cathay Pacific. She started to support her younger sisters and brothers, and supported Mother, too, sending home money when she could.

———————•◆•———————

Mother would hock her jewelry to help pay the mortgage when the rainy season would hit because Father wasn't making any money from logging then either. Sometimes, Mother had to borrow from Grandmother or our aunties. Times were desperate. No one had any money. Everyone was struggling to get by. Then Angie was with Cathay Pacific and she started sending money home to help with the mortgage, and Mother didn't have to go to the pawnshop with her wedding ring and beg them to hold onto it until her next paycheck. It had become a vicious cycle—her hocking it and buying it back—until Angie stepped in with regular money from her job with the airlines.

To this day, Angie still sends money, contributing monthly to the family fund to keep Mom safe and happy. (The rest of us have since joined in as well.)

She flew with the airlines, based in Hong Kong, where she was putting herself through school. She studied hard on the weekends, and then flew on weekdays to support herself. That didn't seem to be enough for Angie, though. She was still mad about Richard getting his schooling paid for, even after she had obtained a bachelor's degree. So she kept going to school, obtaining her MBA. She vowed never to be poor like we were as children. And she accomplished that. She is a true leader. She took the anger that had consumed her over the college fund that was denied her, and she used it to climb mountains.

My sister Jenny, who was child #1, born in 1955, was my first real role model. She was the first person to prepare me for the world. She was big on sharing, caring, and protecting the young ones, always, without fail. Jenny was bilingual, speaking Tamil. And her PR skills had been finely tuned since birth. She was friendly, outgoing, and extremely social. She was the one who gave me all the hugs when Mother was at work. She was Mother's open arms. Anything she had was mine—clothes, food, toys. She was just like a true mother, absolutely selfless—until she was sixteen. That's when she started running away. No one knew why. One day she was helping me study and sewing up a rip in my dress, and the next day she had vanished. We'd always find her, or she'd return, but only to do it again. As you can imagine, Mother and the whole house had no time for shenanigans such as this. There were mouths to feed, trees to tap, floors to sweep, clothes to brush and clean.

Jenny seemed to be possessed. The illness fell upon her so early. Mom and Grandmother decided Jenny had been taken over by black magic. We needed to bring in the big guns to remove the curse.

Bomohs were Muslim healers. Their expertise lied in their in-depth knowledge of medicinal herbs, and they understood the power of mantras (Sanskrit mantras). And *bomahs* are experts in Malay geomancy: the belief that man and the universe are one.

The Malay metaphysical theory states the body and the universe are comprised of the same four elements: fire, water, earth, wind. Illness is caused by an imbalance of these elements. We brought Jenny to a bomoh. We bathed her in cool water with limejuice and filled the area with cedar smoke to rebalance her elements. We prayed, we sang, we cried, we tried everything. Father wasn't around to help. Mom had to be "Mom and Dad" at times like these, dealing with her and all the children's needs. Finally, Jenny was diagnosed with bipolar disorder. It was hard for the family and her too.

Jenny wants to live alone—freedom—but her illness drives her life. Unconditional love, support, and acceptance are our only weapons. All we do now is pray and meditate and send her unconditional love. Only the Divine has the power to heal.

I remember the Jenny before it all changed, the one who was a mother to me. Each Indian and Muslim (Hari Raya) New Year's celebration, I had to promise not to tell Mom (because Mother disliked the celebrations that weren't Chinese), and Jenny would sneak us out to the party. We would be with all our Indian and Muslim friends and neighbors for the grand celebrations. We'd use our hands to eat okra (well, ladies would use their fingers). We'd enjoy bhindi—eggplant, vegetables, fried fish; Rendang—Malay lamb, and chicken curry; muruku—Indian snacks, agar-agar, Jell-O served on banana leaves…there's nothing like home cooked food. Each year we had such a fantastic time. It was a joyous occasion and happiness was all around. Today those celebrations are sweet, secret memories. I promised her not to tell our parents and siblings, and I've stuck to that all these years.

Debbie, sister #2, was second in rank. I admired her like crazy. She was placed by Dad in Canossian Convent since the beginning of primary school, and attended it all the way through secondary school. I envied her respect for school, and the quality of Canossian Convent. It was very strict; there was a big emphasis on discipline. Even as a small child, I knew it was shaping her, for I felt it shaping me as she played a major role in my upbringing. She had all the international nuns (on an exchange program) as her headmistress and teachers. They were all very well trained—from England, Italy, France, etc.

Debbie was kind, worked very hard to help the family without question. She looked after me, especially. She was very patient when it came to my education—going over math again and again. That was my weakest subject, but Debbie had a real talent for it and for the domestic arts. Cooking, baking, sewing—Debbie could do it all. She was an amazing hockey player, and all the teachers liked her very much. Her finesse in sports, in hockey particularly, is what got me thinking about sports in the first place. Prior to that, I hadn't given much consideration to it, given that I was a girl.

Her school had time off in the fall and on Sundays. Debbie would watch TV with me. The Disney Channel was incredible back then. We enjoyed *The Mickey Mouse Show*, Shirley Temple, Donnie and Marie Osmond, *Little House on the Prairie*, *Wonder Woman* and *Six Million Dollar Man*, and *Hawaii 5-0* to name a few.

That's what I remember about Debbie. And, of course, I re-member her putting makeup all over my arm (twice) in the hopes of grabbing onto a dream that had long left the building. She wanted what she thought I wanted for my life, no questions asked. No judgment made. She just wanted happiness for me no matter how unrealistic my dreams were.

Debbie used nearly a bottle of foundation that she had purchased from the nicest department store in the city to try and make that dream possible. Twice.

She was married by that point, the day we painted my arm. We both lived in Kuala Lumpur. Mother said, "You may go find your life, Ah Lian, and you may live in the city near Debbie and her husband, but do not use them as a crutch. Debbie is finding her life too."

This was my preparation for going to find my life—being raised by my sisters: Jenny, Debbie, Angie, and Pau Chu. Watching them grow into different women. Modeling their strengths, praying for the other stuff. And sports. Sports certainly prepared me to work hard, reach goals, surpass goals, and be part of a team. It prepared me for failure. And success. "Great…" Mother would say, glancing briefly at my medal before getting back to work…. Sometimes success is a whisper not a scream. Sometimes it's not about the medal.

I was ready, I guess. I was of age. In many ways, I had less than most—living on the plantation, saving pennies for food, fighting for floor space by the window, washing clothes so that there were clothes, never seeing Father, tapping trees at dawn. And then there was my arm: I was leaving home with a terrible secret hidden under the sleeve of my blouse, the kind that you risk death to keep hidden. That's how I still felt about it back then.

But in different ways, I had so much more. I was leaving my home, my nest, with a good education. I knew I was loved. I had people rooting for my success. I had a strong foundation in several faiths. I had skills. I was a hard worker, and honesty came easy. I did not have much of an ego left, but that would later prove to be advantageous. I had birds of paradise, monkeys swinging from trees, the roosters crowing at dawn, wild boar as jungle rivals and excellent dinner "companions." I had sunshine, heat, warm rain on my cheeks reminding me that life is about moments. There were shiny rubber tree seeds in my pocket representing the power and beauty of growth. They were my diamonds. And I had stopped crying myself to sleep, and started to believe in…something. I didn't know what that something was. I didn't know what my future life looked like, but thanks to Mother, Father, Angie, Jenny, Debbie, Pau Chu, and Sister Dorothy, I was not afraid to close my eyes and walk forward.

Mostly, I was leaving with Mother's voice in my heart, my soul, and my head. She reminded me of right and wrong. She embodied faith. She steered my future like she was the sole conductor. That voice in my head made me feel safe, as safe as a girl with only one good arm could feel.…

I had an incredible childhood, if you think about it. I didn't have to work as much as the others. I wasn't given to another family and forced to escape and find my way home without shoes. I literally won the lotto when it came to school. I was so lucky to receive a beautiful education at the Canossian Convent School. My backyard was a real, live jungle—hundreds of acres of wild plants, flowers, trees, animals, a thousand beautiful creatures singing to me "good morning." The rain was good. It was warm. It was for bathing, drinking, playing, survival. The sun was strong. I had those diamonds in my pocket. They were priceless to me—the reason for everything. They were the reason I had anything at all. My arm brought panic, but sports? Well, when sports came into my life, I learned that a beautiful and perfect looking arm wasn't everything. When I threw the shot putt, no one stared at the scars on my arm. Their eyes followed the path of the ball. And then they cheered. They always cheered more loudly than I thought my throw deserved.

My childhood has been blessed.

It's perspective, I guess....

c h a p t e r   s i x

"Everyone wants a perfect ending. But over the years, I've learned that some of the best poems don't rhyme, and many great stories don't have a clear beginning, middle, or end. Life is about not knowing, embracing change, and taking a moment and making the best of it without knowing what's going to happen next."

—Ritu Ghatourey

LIFE IS A MILLION moments; that's been ingrained since birth. But these situations, these occurrences, these stories that end up as memories can vary greatly in degree and impact. I was faced with another big moment in 1984: I was leaving home. I was terrified, truthfully. I didn't have a realistic dream any longer, just a destination: Kuala Lumpur. I wasn't certain of the kind of work I would find, or of my skills, which were average at best. Mother assured me I was wrong about that. She said it's not all about brains and solving equations; it's about honesty and the desire and ability to work hard. She said I had always gotten straight As in those departments. That helped. Then she said that I'd better have some fast fun before I get down to the business of living, of surviving, of facing my unknown destiny head on. It was a time to celebrate my accomplishments thus far, and take a breather, too. The money in the red envelope from my father, aunts and uncles, other relatives, and elderly friends of the family wasn't enough for college, but it was something.... And so I did what other kids did. I went backpacking!

There were three of us. I went on this adventure with my best friends from Canossian Convent School: Chow and Loh. Both of them were top science students. (Yes, they had helped me study on more than one occasion.) Our friendships had grown stronger over the last six years. The three of us took the same bus to and from school. That bus ride was nearly one hour each way, which gave us ample opportunity to chat about sports, social issues, siblings. We didn't much talk about boys. No one was allowed to date boys, so we kept that chatter to a minimum. *Why tempt ourselves?* We'd solve unfinished math or schoolwork problems on the bus. Chow and Loh always found time to solve my math problems. They were sweet like that, and they were smartest friends I had. They flew through their coursework like they knew all the answers before the questions were asked. They graduated at the top of our class. Both Chow and Loh were pursuing a higher education at different universities. They were certain about that, just as I knew for sure that Kuala Lumpur was where my future would begin, after two wonderful weeks of bonding and backpacking, that is. Although our paths were to split hard and fast in fourteen short days, we were young, energetic, in love with life, hungry for knowledge, ready to explore and to embark on the

University of Life together for a brief moment in time. Even then, we knew how precious our final two weeks together would be. And we were so happy being friends. I wondered how I'd ever find friends like that again. It would be two decades before I ever did.... I'm glad I didn't know that then.

While backpacking, we discussed everything under the sweet warm sky, including boys. We talked about what our future boy-friends would be like (and our future husbands). When we'd exhaust that subject, daily, we'd move on, speculating about accomplishments once we were to enter the real world, as if this hiking trip was a fantasy, or some kind of world that paralleled the other one. Chow and Loh's university education felt more certain and more structured. No one knew what I was in for. I explained how my family only had enough money for one child to go to college, and how that money went to brother #1. I was #9. Even if siblings 1, 2, and 3 turned down the college fund, it would still have to get passed up by 5, 6, 7, and 8 before it got to me. To my relief, they said it was exciting, my unpredictable journey. They convinced me of it, saying I was the lucky one. Lucky Number Nine, that's what they called me. At that point, everyone who knew us had our number system down. Chow said, "You wait and see, Ah Lian, you're going to rule the earth and the sky. You'll be a goddess."

Loh added, "You're going to the University of Life to be a sky goddess! I'm just going to be a school teacher. How boring."

We laughed so hard after that.

We went for an Indian dinner one night. It was our banana leaves dinner, and, yes, we used our hands. We walked along Serangoon Road, a famous Indian Street in Singapore. Lots of Indian buildings of worship along with Chinese temples and Muslim mosques were built on this street. The shop houses were eighteenth century in design. Architecturally speaking, they were breathtaking. This part of town was called Little India. A lot of the shops specializing in "everything Indian" had been erected the last half of the century—vendors were selling *sari* (Indian fabric used to create colorful dresses), biryani rice and coconut candies, masala tea and macadamia ice cream, and Indian-style wooden furniture. The city was rich with culture. We walked day and night continuing to window shop on Orchard Road in Singapore.

Orchard Road is the busiest, most expensive, and most elaborately decorated road in all of the country. This road, and the main shopping mall, was where all the folks flocked during Christmastime. Even just watching passersby with their shopping bags—heavy in their right hand, even heavier bags in the left—made us feel both envious and exhilarated. We were envious with wonder at how those people had so much money (and time) to shop shop shop. And we were exhilarated because, well, someday that would be us. Teenage girls are real dreamers, especially when they all get together.

As backpackers, we also visited Sentosa Island where we went to the beach and caught tans. Sentosa was really much smaller back then, and most of the island was covered in green vegetation. We took a cable car there. I can't really recall the ride itself, apart from remembering the floor of the cabin was transparent. We saw great views of the sea underneath our feet and the lush beauty surrounding the island. Once we arrived, we bought a package of tickets that included admission to all major attractions on the island. Our first stop was the wax museum, known as Images of Singapore. There were four zones that were themed Festivals of Singapore, Surrender Chamber, Pioneers of Singapore, and a multimedia show. One of the most memorable exhibitions was the Surrender Chamber. They had the actual mockup of the surrender of the Japanese to the British after a two-yearlong occupation of Singapore. Then we took a quick turn to get a close-up look at the Merlion. That's a giant stone sculpture of a lion with a fish's body. The Merlion is considered the mascot of Singapore. Our next stop was the F, the Fountain Gardens—a set of exquisitely designed gardens that were fashioned after the Gardens of Versailles. The Garden was split into four quadrants with elaborately detailed stone fountains along the main axis. You could see the Merlion off in the distance, watching over us, with nothing but green in the foreground. It's sad that this vista is now gone and replaced by the sheltered canopies of Resorts World Sentosa, which has completely blocked the Merlion from view. Now, there's Disneyland. The theme park was finally erected. Today it is one of the busiest tourist resort-casino destinations in the Pacific Rim Asia, and in the world. Sentosa has always had the reputation of being a crime free island. We were free to travel on our shoestring budget with ease.

What we had hoped for—an epic adventure before we all buck-led down—was now a reality. Experiencing Singapore came at a perfect time for us all. When we finally ended back home in Kluang with our last three-hour train ride and we stopped at the Malaysia-Singapore customs border to get our passports stamped, we felt different, renewed, older, wiser. *How did Mother know that two weeks backpacking with a couple math geeks would turn me into a woman?* We were ready for a new phase in our lives. We were no longer high school girls. We were young women. It was at this border that we bid each other farewell, and hoped and prayed that fate would bring us back to one another again very soon. I promised to visit them at their universities. They promised to spend a weekend in our country's capital with me. We went on and on…. Those bear hugs we shared that day were mixed with bittersweet emotions. Chow teared up, then Loh and I followed. It got real silly. At one point, I remembered thinking: *My goodness, Ah Lian, get a hold of yourself; your friends are only moving a couple of hours away. It will be like it always was.*

Looking back, I was thankful for our dramatic, drawn out depar-ture, and all the gushing at the train station, for that was the last time we ever saw each other.

Jungle Life

The Early Years 1953-1982

Mother and Father's Engagement Photo, 1953

Front: Angie, Pau Chu, Ah Lian, Charles, Richard

Back: Jenny, Mom, Debbie, 1970

Ah Lian, Christmas, Kluang, Malaysia, 1972

Front: Charles, Jason, Ah Lian, Pau Chu
Back: Jenny, Siew Ying, Angie, Richard, Debbie
Kluang, Malaysia, 1971

Mom and Debbie Tapping Rubber Trees, Kluang, Malaysia, 1970s

Front: Ah Lian, Mother, Healer Grandmother, Father, Jason

Back: Pau Chu, Debbie, Siew Ying, Jenny, Richard, Angie, Charles

Lucky Garden, Kluang, Malaysia, 1975

Chinese Chong Hwa School 1, Kluang, Malaysia 1976

Ah Lian, Flute Band Uniform, Kluang, Malaysia, 1976

Left: Ah Lian—Red House Captain, Kluang, Malaysia, 1982

Left: Ah Lian—Red House Captain and Team

Kluang, Malaysia, 1982

Red House Wins for Number of Awards

Ah Lian, Captain Award, Kluang, Malaysia, 1982

Canossian Convent Leadership Training Program

Port Dickson, Malaysia, 1980

Mr. Loganathan, "Coach" of the Volleyball Team

Champions, Sekolah Tinggi, Kluang, 1983

Climbing Gunung Lambak Mountain Day Trip with Girlfriends
Kluang, Malaysia, 1982

chapter seven

People with nine as their lucky number can hardly be successful unless they act upon their dreams with focused action.

YOU DIDN'T NEED MUCH as a young single person moving to the capital of Kuala Lumpur. I mean, you needed money, but I was able to find a place quickly, sleeping in a room with two other girls. Establishing my first residence in Malaysia's capital was pulled off with ease. Girls fresh out of high school could room together to get by and save good money while learning how to grow up and live the city life.

One of the older girls from the convent school, Lillian, a volleyball teammate of mine, was a secretary for a very important businessman. It was pure luck that I had decided to contact her. She was looking for a personal assistant, a Gal Friday. She hired me on the spot. My athletic abilities and connections landed my first real job. It was like Mom said: the skills I had were working to help me discover my true destiny.

I had many tasks as the "assistant to the assistant," like answering the phone, making coffee for our boss, typing up letters. I worked in the mailroom—opening all mail, filing, sending Telex (faxes) to America and Hong Kong. I was so nervous. This wasn't like tapping rubber trees, where my real purpose was to spend time with Mom, and she was the responsible party, the one in charge of everything. I had responsibilities. My hands broke out in cold sweats all day long for the first two months. I started out as a slow typist, with my two-finger routine. I was so nervous that someone would say something. Some letters took me half the day before I got all the words in all the right spots. You can imagine. I had to organize two sheets of paper with carbon paper on it (to ensure I sent out one letter and kept one copy for filing). That was in addition to getting the words right. In those days, the electrical typewriter had both red and black colored ribbon. I made so many mistakes. Retyping and using so much paper and carbon copies over and over was wasteful, but there was no better solution. Sometimes the Telex to the US and Hong Kong took two hours to get ready. Everything was alien to me. I had no clue what secretarial or clerical work entailed when I agreed to take the job. Lillian couldn't have possibly known that she hired someone with no knowledge of the industry. *Could she?* Daily, I'd say to my girlfriend, "Please have patience, and teach me all that you know." I counted my blessings just as often. Then I'd hear the words, "*Jumpa esok ya,*" and breathe a sigh of relief. ("See you tomorrow" in Bahasa Malaysia.) I made it through another day. Lillian was so kind, patient, supportive. She encouraged me, and assured me I was doing fine.

74

When our boss dictated and she wrote in shorthand, oh, how I envied her. What speed. I felt like a bean sprout during dictation by comparison. She was the most efficient and impressive personal assistant anyone could ask for. And Lillian could detect when I was stressed like no other (except the one who had given birth to me, of course). No sooner did I feel the tears climbing into my eyes, and there she was, by my side, assisting her own assistant. Keeping deadlines and order in the office was the name of the game, but even above that, she wanted to make sure I was okay. She'd find me in the ladies' room some days, doing my deep meditative breathing. This was before I knew how to do it effectively. In fact, it wasn't deep breathing at all. Looking back, it was that thing that happens right before an anxiety attack: panic. I'd be on the toilet with all my clothes still on, just breathing, trying to unwind or relax. This would go on until I felt lightheaded, ready to collapse. She kept up the encouragement, even on those days. "Try harder, practice more typing at home. And study old letters to learn the boss's handwriting."

That was cryptic to say the least. My boss should have been a doctor; his handwriting was that unreadable. One time, Lillian was out sick. I was in zombie mode the whole day taking over Lillian's responsibilities, and taking care of our boss. It was so tense. I had to go "meditate" in the ladies' room five times that day. Four of those times were before lunch!

Even though I was only two and a half hours from home by public transport, Kuala Lumpur was a different world. Busy and noisy with the constant bustle of people, and filthy too. The air was thick with pollution. Each time I was on a bus, we were packed in like sardines, body to body, no space to move an inch…as everyone wanted to make room so no one was late for work. (It is the capital of Malaysia…what do you expect?) Some stranger didn't shower, someone didn't brush his or her teeth, someone overdosed on perfume, your basic body odor—it was bad news on the bus for my nose, every single time. This was the opposite of the lifestyle in Kluang, which was relaxed. Every day was Sunday in Kluang compared to city life. There were a lot of folks on motorcycles, saving time and getting to work faster. They were noisy, and weaved in and out of the buses and cabs. It was hectic but exciting to be a part of it.

I didn't know the girls I roomed with, but it didn't take long to figure out that I wouldn't be developing any lifelong friendships. There was no backpacking trip in our future. If I didn't keep an eye on my money, shoes, shirts, favorite jeans, jewelry…they'd be gone. One time my actual bankcard was stolen. The card itself. I don't know how they knew my special pin number, but it must not have been very clever, maybe my birthdate. Anyway, one of my roommates took the card and helped herself to the money right out of my savings. It was devastating the first time the thieving occurred. I had been naïve. Lesson number one: Everyone wasn't raised by Thu Ah Nim. Don't trust strangers just because they look like any other nice girl (just because they looked like…me). That wasn't the worst of it. I only had a few shirts and blouses. Those meant more than even the pennies in the bank. Because of my arm, my shirts were special. They were designed to hide my secret, and keep me safe. Try explaining that to a thief. They don't come equipped with a bunch of sympathy, that's the thing about most strangers. I don't know, maybe if they had known about my arm, they would have steered clear of the blouses. Maybe. I never thought to mention it.

Learning to survive started early in my country's capital. I had to be more careful with my money and all my personal possessions.

I made 250-300 ringgits a month. It wasn't much. Frugal became my middle name. Rina "Frugal" Tham. It had a nice ring to it. I didn't eat all that much, so that helped. Breakfast, rent, bus fare, dinners—that's where all my money went, and then into my savings. I didn't party. It wasn't for me.

After one year at the secretarial position (where I was the assistant to the assistant), the assistant, Lillian, was offered a bigger position with more responsibility and a higher salary. This was with another company, so Lillian resigned. I left shortly thereafter. I didn't see myself as being ready and capable of tackling her job. I was typing with at least four of my fingers by then, but I still had to stare straight at the keys to do it. This resulted in no more than twenty words per minute, which was hardly enough to be called competent. It's a big world out there, time to plunge back into it again, time to learn a new trade. That's what my intuition told me.

———◆———

It was Christmas Day, 1984. I had never ever lost control of myself, except for when those nurses scrubbed my arm at dawn when I was in the hospital. Yet there I was, shivering and crying. I was babbling. I sounded like a kid who was wailing for ice cream after his parents had delivered a firm no. It was a genuine breakdown, with tears streaming out of control. They were warming my face like the Malaysian rain. I felt like I couldn't move my legs or arms. They were numb, weak. I could flop them here, and flop them there, but I had no muscle control. It was terrifying. I was experiencing something I had never experienced before: I was dead drunk. I was collapsed, sprawled out on top of the bar, and drunk as a skunk. I had just finished my first (and last) beer ever. And that was that. Thank goodness it was the holiday, because business was slow. Even though my legs were flippy and floppy and numb, my heart was beating fast. I thought it might bust through my chest like it was running the last leg in a neck-in-neck relay race. My lungs worked to expand to catch more oxygen, but I couldn't seem to take in enough of it. I was panicking again, like I had done at my assistant to the assistant job. My friends arrived right before I went into this real "melty" state. Just as I was about to slide off the barstool like hot wax down the edge of a candle, they got on either side and propped me up. Then they warmed me up by covering me with blankets, I think. *Maybe they covered me with their coats…?* It took two hours to recover enough to walk out of the place. They dripped hot lemon juice steadily into my mouth. I remembered feeling the embarrassment of "tomorrow" looming over my head as I did my best to follow their instructions on sobering up. That was the worst experience ever. It's almost a shame I remember it so clearly.

The evening started out pretty simple: I was at a bar, waiting. It was just the bartender and me. He was young, about my age, friendly, and attractive. I remember him having a very nice smile. We hit it off, and he convinced me to try a special drink they had. It was a new kind of beer, a porter. It was supposed to be the latest and greatest. And it was just beer, after all; that's what he said. I practically lived in nightclubs for my new job by that point. Yet, I had never tried alcohol. I wasn't driving. Didn't own a car. Chalk it up to new experiences, I agreed to try the porter. This story probably sounds silly to most people, but somewhere inside me, I knew that alcohol wasn't going to be my thing. But like many young people starting off in the world, I felt pressure to fit in, to try new things, to do what everyone else did. I thought I ought to try a beer. That porter was confusing from beginning to end. Bitter. Thick. Chalky. It was the opposite of powdered coffee, which was always strong but so smooth and delightful. I suffered through it. That should have told me something. The voice in my head knew my body was rejecting every drop, yet I forged on, cringing and drinking. This porter tasted like…nothing I could think of. It didn't remind me of home, or of my future. I couldn't connect it to anything I knew, not the smell of a jungle flower, not a spice for cooking, nothing. It was foreign. I was so focused on the taste, texture, and smell of this new thing from my new world that I forgot to consider the effects it might have. Next thing I knew I was dizzy. Then I got swept up by melancholy. God only knows over what. I wasn't old enough to have a big life to cry about. I knew people with big, hard lives—mother came to mind—

but I didn't have one of them. Not yet. I didn't have an absent husband, or nine kids, or anything like that. I hadn't even experienced my first broken heart. That didn't seem to matter. Once that porter made its way into my veins, it must have kept going, right up to my eyes, where it found a quick exit. It came out in tears, streams of tears. And then my legs got flippy and floppy…and you know the rest.

That was my first and last experience with alcohol. We were not to be friends, alcohol and I. Lesson learned the hard way. That was also the day that I learned a little humiliation goes a long way with me. Some people, they don't mind it so much. I don't mind hard work. I don't have to always be right. I don't mind failing if I know I did my best. But being humiliated? That emotion is for the birds.

A string of positions doing accounting for clubs came along after I left Lillian, my friend from volleyball. Girls my age made good money being escorts for businessmen at dinner clubs. If they were very good at entertaining, they made lots of money. I was a "behind the scenes" kind of girl. I kept record of all these business activities. I was not the girl dining with the men who had endless amounts of money to blow. That part was amazing, though. Sometimes the bill would be in the thousands. I would see the slips and have to record everything in the company books. These luxuries were claimed as "business entertainment expenses." A bottle of whiskey for two thousand dollars was a "business" expense. The girls made lots of money from being pretty, and from being friendly, too. They were paid hourly, plus they earned commission on the drinks they pushed, which explained the two- to ten-thousand-dollar bottles of whiskey on the bills. I can't imagine there's a big difference in tastes once they reach a certain price. Two thousand dollars? Ten thousand dollars? Doesn't it all taste like liquid gold after a certain point? I used to wonder. I certainly hoped they tasted superior to that porter....

While I'd organize the books from the prior night's festivities, it always felt like I was on the outside of that kind of beauty—the beauty that persuaded men to spend thousands of dollars on one bottle of whiskey. I'd try envisioning the evening, but the images blended like my mind's eye was looking through a kaleidoscope, like I could barely focus on any one thing. Images spun in my head—fast, colorful, too much for my senses. Sometimes it hurt a little, trying to picture what it'd be like to be a pretty girl on a businessman's arm. I'd see one coming to work, as I was going home. We were not the same species. I was a wild boar, she a flying monkey. I was a grass-hopper, she a purple butterfly. Even though I had no clue what my future was to look like, I was certain it wasn't about painting my lips red and wearing silky dresses for strange men, or about laughing at their jokes, which I rarely understood. (The ones I did catch onto, I didn't find to be too humorous, truth be told.) Doing the books was closer to my destiny than pretending to laugh—a thing I had never worked to master before. Plus, I was a morning person, and that job worked late into the night. Even just rummaging through the bills and the expenses was exhausting. Momentary envy would fill my veins when I saw the commissions on the Chevas Regal Royal Salute aged fifty years. Mother has kept me honest, so I was able to admit that to myself, about my envy. After all, the commissions from selling one bottle of Chevas Regal Royal would have paid my rent for six months. But, that emotion was short-lived. It was on par with humiliation. I had no real time for it.

After two years of bookkeeping, I left that position and all my young friends. Even though I wasn't a pretty girl whose future seemed foggy beyond her long, lush eyelashes, my career was feeling stagnant, like it was going sideways. I always felt forward motion at the convent school. Each year was more challenging than the last. Every new track season came with more records to beat. Sure, some of them were my own—the records I was up against—but it was a concrete opportunity to excel. I could no longer see the point of being the bookkeeper at the men's club. I didn't understand "whose time I was trying to beat." I felt like I was sitting in the same place, taking in the same view. The silky dresses, good food, beautiful Gucci handbags, and high-heeled shoes—they were nice, but not for me. Maybe it was my vulnerability from the scar, maybe it was the voice of my mother in my head—*be honest, be wise, be strong, stand tall.* Maybe this was not my cup of tea. Sometimes things are that simple. Earlier in my life, before I left home, I remembered feeling that I was supposed to work hard to find my destiny—that was going to be my plan. Work hard. This inability to perceive my future, even just a slice of it, combined with the feeling that I was the oldest twenty-one-year-old in all of Kuala Lumpur, became too much to bear.

Ultimately, I resigned.

Within the week, I found an opening. I was hired to work as an assistant to a successful, local entrepreneur, Mr. Ng. I sold memberships at his full service club. It was my job to recruit members to use the facility and all it had to offer. The first thing that was dazzling upon entering the Sungei Mas Club was the rows upon rows of one-armed bandits. That's what you saw when you came in the main entrance. That's what you heard, too. Snooker was big there. That's a game on a billiard table played with pool sticks and balls, similar to pool. There were also pool tables. Pool is a game played on a billiard table with pool sticks and balls, similar to snooker. (I hope that covers everybody.) There were also snack bars and regular bars for drinking. There was a beautiful gym, a facility for exercising complete with locker rooms. A stage for the live performances was the main attraction. DJs setup their turntables there. This place was fully functioning.

I was trained to be an organizer. Actually, that training started back at convent school. Despite my C average, I was always quite organized. I planned the club's promotions to encourage members to spend money to use the gym and showers, to stay for happy hour or aerobic classes, or to gamble. Let's face it, feeding the slot machines brought in nice revenue. Sometimes, the guests and members won on those one-armed bandits too. I saw the lucky ones win lots of money. Those slots were hot. I think because there were so many winners, and the economy was thriving in Malaysia like it never had, it seemed okay to me then, the gambling. Happiness was all around.

Mr. Ng personally trained me to be a promotional manager. I became comfortable speaking on a stage in front of dozens, and eventually, hundreds of people. Believe it or not, that's a talent. My skills for detail became very refined; they had to. The pace of this job and all the promoting was fast and constant. A constant stream of activities was key for success. I had to get innovative after a few months. I started creating social gatherings where prizes were given away. Plenty of money was spent by simply attending these awards shows and giveaways. That's when I learned that giving a little away seemed to bring in revenue tenfold.

The most unforgettable event I organized was when I launched a famous pop song artist's tour, Ms. Cally Kwan, right there at the club. She came all the way from Hong Kong. We had a full house. The tickets were sold out within hours of the announcement. It was the most money we had ever brought in from one event. Alcohol sales were at an all-time high.

Mr. Ng was so thrilled he purchased two tickets for my colleague and me to go to Hong Kong for a week's vacation as a complimentary token of his true appreciation from securing Cally Kwan in concert. Hong Kong was nice, but not for me. I was grateful for the trip, and even gladder I didn't have to live there.

Not long after that, Mr. Ng left the club. He was offered a higher salary to work for a bigger company. After about three months, I was hired to work at the headquarters, the How Par building on Jalan Ismail. The position came with a raise, and extra responsibility. My main job was to oversee all the clubs' promotional activities. There were about a dozen of them in full swing at the time. I was a liaison and negotiator, in charge of the in-house advertisement. We had to put events in the local newspapers. The promotion of the clubs was ongoing, so ads were always being created and improved upon. There was no cap on how many members the clubs could have. That was exciting and exhausting. The exhausting part was that we had to be constantly innovative, always topping our last great marketing scheme. Alcohol was a big part of the marketing tactics. Alcohol and gambling were big draws, and the club's main source of income, just like with the bars and local restaurants. An important discovery was made at this job: I was born with a green thumb, the kind that grows money for a company.

I couldn't have been at this position for more than six months when I was offered another position overseeing the advertising and promotional programming staff for all the clubs throughout Malaysia. Twenty clubs. I was in charge of raising revenue for twenty Malaysian entertainment/health clubs.

Now I was planning modeling shows with a runway and everything. The people of Malaysia really have a thing for fashion. I hired an *Umpapa* group from Copenhagen during Oktoberfest. Their music is very rhythmic, focusing on the brass instruments. It's hypnotic. We had a magic show. Michael Jackson breakdancing competitions. Best dressed contests. Beauty contests. Singing competitions in which awards were given out to members only. *Datuk Sheikh*, who sang Tom Jones' covers and was big in France releasing his first *single*, *"Tu Sais Je T'aime (You Know I Love You")*, was an immense hit.

Any famous musicians were sure to be a huge success. And if you booked one great band or singer, others tended to follow.

Karaoke was big. As many of you know, it's been all the rage in Asian countries since the seventies. In the sixties Minus-one Music was being created in the Philippines. That was when a song was recorded twice and released for purchase. The first recording was regular, by that I mean with the vocals. Then the second song was released but it was just instrumental so that people could sing on their own to it. I used to sing along, loving the second releases. Like running a marathon, singing karaoke expelled my stress. But this remedy only took seconds to take effect, which was delightful.

A few years after that, in 1971, in Kobe, Japan, a musician by the name of Daisuke Inoue created a machine that played his original tunes (songs with a nice drum beat) if one inserted a yen. He then leased out these machines all over the land. They wound up in restaurants, bars, hotels. It was considered an upscale form of entertainment.

Karaoke was huge in Malaysia, and all of Asia by the early eighties. (It wouldn't be until the nineties that it would start to sweep the US.) Mime competitions were big, too. We had lots of karaoke and mime contests. I'd schedule monthly shows and they'd always be sold out.

This job was fun, like my first job (assisting) was nerve racking, and my second job (bookkeeping) was exhausting. Every day at this job, I had a reason to smile. Fortunately, I never had to hide in a bathroom stall. There was lots of travel, lots of long hours ensuring the shows I planned were executed successfully from beginning to end. There was a ton of strategizing, and some anxiety came with that. But when the shows sold out, a great feeling of accomplishment would wash over me.

I was often working well into the night. I wasn't flying in the friendly skies, but I was having genuine opportunities to see some of the world, meet different kinds of people, and it seemed like I was on a path toward some kind of dream. I made it home annually for the Chinese New Year. I used one of my two weeks' vacation time for that, and would backpack around Singapore, Thailand, Indonesia, and Sri-Lanka for the second week.

At the age of twenty-two, my position changed yet again. I had been so successful at booking talent for these clubs that I was put in charge of finding new talent. The clubs were evolving in every way. They were gaining a big reputation for success. I was sent across the country and continent in search of working girls. I became a talent scout. We needed new blood to perform in singing and dancing shows, musicals, burlesque shows, acrobatic shows, and we needed every kind of showgirl. They sent me to Thailand and Johor Bahru to look for pretty girls with special talents. I was also in search of exceptionally beautiful models to work wherever they were needed. I was given a bodyguard as a full-time companion to this special assignment. You know, there were gangsters overlooking their territories. But, overall, I played the role of a smooth operator, and more success would be soon to follow.

At first, this new position was awkward. Walking into random clubs in different countries and posing as a talent scout was tricky business. I was digging for the next star. No one wants to let go of his best girls. It was challenging for me to talk to strangers in the clubs. Stating my purpose was just plain strange. It's not like I was hanging out in high schools watching basketball games looking for the next Michael Jordan. People weren't scouting back then like I was. In many ways, I didn't fit in visually. This wasn't about my arm. Even though I was young, I really looked out of place in a hot club late at night. It was obvious I came in for a reason. I had "I'm on a mission" written all over me. I was all business in my long-sleeved blouses buttoned up to my chin. Fortunately, my face was kind, and the owners and managers were mostly nice. And they warmed up quite easily to the idea that their club could be the place where a "star" could be discovered.

I kept it simple for the first trip, and went where it seemed I might land a few great finds without too much resistance. This was in Thailand. I was able to return home with a handful of very talented and versatile transvestites. The second crop of talent I brought from Johore Bahru to Kuala Lumpur. They sang in Mandarin, Bahasa Malaysia, and English. To find talented artists that were multi-lingual was almost unheard of.

I was promoted tout de suite to the main headquarters, thanks to the talents of these great performers. It started to blow my mind that other people's talents were launching my career. I was sure feeling lucky, like Chow and Loh had predicted. Twenty more clubs were added to my list of things to do. I'd work all day, creating ads and setting up promotions, then go home and take a power nap, and then return at dark to manage the performances at night. I was extremely thankful for my good health and natural endurance once I made it to this position, which was, at times, intellectually intense and physically laborious. I learned from this job that a little stress, just like fear, is good for the soul. But just a little bit.

Of course, the club's environment was crowded, smoky, noisy, hot, and sweaty. There was usually a live band playing or solo artist singing. As much as I loved setting up the acts, my favorite place to be was not inside the clubs. At times, some members wanted me to drink with them. In Asian culture you must drink and smoke with the customers, otherwise they'll view it as rude and disrespectful. They truly expect it. Knowing I can't, or don't, like drinking or smoking was not acceptable. *"That's no excuse, Rina. People need to feel respected."* I could hear her voice. Therefore, I had to set up a system. In order to make all the customers happy, I'd fake the drinking part. The bartenders and I were in cahoots. All my drinks were black, just like Guinness Stout, but in actuality, I was drinking Guinness Malta. We were doing our own magic show. It was a good trick. Pretending to be able to drink kept our loyal customers, well, loyal. And they were happy, as they felt like I was one of them, like we were bonding. If I can drink with them, they can trust me; this much I knew. I've always had respect for Chinese culture and for tradition, but not so much so that I would risk my own health and my career for it.

I was feeling validated for the first time in a long time, like I was being judged for my capabilities. Making a good living, being in charge of my destiny, mingling with other successful business people, feeling like I was making a difference somewhere, being so busy I didn't have time to contemplate life or my future too much—this was freedom. It was my first real taste of a life that was being designed by my every next move. This wasn't a four-year college degree, but it felt just as valuable.

Some days, I wasn't sure I had the brains, the beauty, or the stamina to make it through another six-hour day and eight-hour night, but I plugged on, and did my best, for this was my destiny for that moment. Putting my whole heart into it, into anything and everything has always been the goal. And living with awareness, that was essential, too, even if that meant pulling off a few magic tricks. The alternative to the magic trick would have meant losing business, or more humiliation with floppy legs. I wasn't going there.

I never confessed that it was Guinness Malta with fresh limejuice all those years, not as long as I was working in club promotions. I just drank my special potion, and smiled like everyone else.

chapter eight

I KNEW OF THE story of Never Never Land from watching Disney. All children knew that magical story with Peter Pan. But as much as I liked watching fairy tales, I didn't believe in them. My life was far from a fairy tale. That's how all the great stories went, though. They started out tough, and ended with a rainbow. I've always had a constant stream of hope pumping through my veins, and I liked my life; it was mine, after all.

Even though believing in fairy tales seemed silly, having hope did not.

Never Never Land was originally just called Never Never. It was a region in the Outback that was completely unexplored. People said to never go there, thus the name. It was remote, far off, scary, the unknown. That's what my father had been to me for most my life. He was far away, frightening, unknown, a mystery. By the time I was twenty-five, I had seen success, and I had found love. I was a very happy person. My arm hadn't stopped me from succeeding in business, or in my personal life. In fact, when people noticed it they appeared more curious than anything. Children would say, "What happened?" And they'd point, but it was innocent curiosity. A simple explanation, the truth, satisfied them, and they moved onto the next attention grabber—candy from their mama's purse, a puppy passing by—always living right in the moment like children do.

This came as a pleasant surprise, a huge relief, and was an interesting life lesson. The only person truly concerned about the look of my arm all these years…was me. This was valuable insight: I wasn't giving people enough credit. The tale of my life was beginning to look bright. The rainbow was peeking through the rain.

Still, something was missing. I felt this pull to know my father. *Was it the father-daughter connection?* Maybe. My father was alive, and yet, I didn't know the first thing about him. I didn't think that once I had a connection to my dad, my life would be perfect. It's mostly that an opportunity was passing me by every day I ignored the inner pull. I was saying "no" to the chance to learn and grow. That wasn't like me at all.…

I had always thought of Dad in relation to Mom. That always gave me a knot in my stomach. I hurt for her. I sometimes felt anger, and then I'd brush it off, for it wasn't really my own. I remembered his strict and sometimes uncalled for disciplinary actions. Was it him? Was it his mother, my grandmother, who provoked that? And then there were my two stepsisters born of my mother's sister. There were girlfriends. He had one girlfriend in particular. They were victims of his actions, too, I guess. Still, over the years, when thoughts of my father entered my head, my feelings shifted from anger and heaviness to that pull. I began to feel like there was a rope knotted around my heart with the other end tied around Indonesia. It was a tug of war: me against Never Never Land, the island where my father lived.

But there was one obstacle. As I said, I had found love.

My boyfriend, Peter, an engineer, was a nice and caring man, and well educated. We loved each other very much. We were so compatible, and conversation came easy. Neither of us were the fighting types, and we did not have jealousy issues. We dated just like any other adults. Together we'd visit our families during Chinese New Year, respectively. We had been together two years now. Our parents didn't get too involved in our relationship, as Chinese parents have been known to do. We didn't talk of marriage, so they gave us some distance. I'd call our relationship comfortable. Realizing that that word sounds boring, I wish there were a better one to describe what Peter and I had, but I can't think of it. Comfort can be a good thing. I could see us heading toward marriage, just not right away.

One day, when the desire to move to Indonesia overwhelmed me and I was breathing fast and shallow, like back when I was the assistant to the assistant, I took that as a sign and resigned from work. I had saved quite a bit by this point. It was time to go to Indonesia and get to know my dad.

I spoke to Peter about this immediately. He was the first person I told. It could have been a mistake, not discussing this with him prior to handing in my resignation. It seemed like when I confessed to the urgency that had been haunting me, stalking me more and more each day, he didn't relate. I felt a little foolish after that, but still quite determined. He was reluctant about letting me go. I was presenting my dilemma in a way that encouraged and included him, even though it wasn't his decision, and didn't technically include him.

I did love him.

I didn't want to leave him.

But I had to make this trip.

Those were the facts.

After talking to Peter, I paid a visit to Mom. She's never been shy about expressing herself. She was the perfect person to go to for counsel. My mom commented that we were just dating and not married yet, which meant I was free to do anything I desired. That was her translation of my situation.

"I am grateful for my home and my job and my life with Peter. But my father.... I don't even know if he drinks coffee or tea in the morning. Or what his favorite books are, if he has any at all. And he doesn't know mine.

Sun Tzu (孫子—pinyin: Sūnzǐ) is an honorific title bestowed upon Sūn Wu (孫武 c. 544-496 BC), the author of *The Art of War* (孫子兵法). This was my favorite book—an immensely influential ancient Chinese book on military strategy. Sun Tzu believed in the use of the military sciences to effect outcomes that would result in peace. I often thought, I bet Dad read this book. I'd love to talk to him about it. My father was a real seeker of knowledge.

I was confused, for I was comfortable in Kuala Lumpur, with my friends and at the University of Life. It had been good to me. I

94

was flourishing. But I feared regret. "One day, it'll be too late. I will have many things, but I won't have memories of him."

"You need to follow your heart, Ah Lian. I have at least taught you that much."

"But…."

"But, Peter will be there."

She always knew what I was going to say.

"If Peter really loves you, Ah Lian, he should give you all the support you need, and understand your heart, and wait for you to return. It is but two years. Two years in terms of true love is nothing. Sometimes a double shift tapping trees feels like two years. Sometimes a good night's sleep does, or a long rain, or a ride to the city on the train. It takes some children two years to talk, then once they do, it's like they've always known words. It's nothing. It's easy."

I didn't know about all that, but she always liked her points to be strong.

"It is good to do it now and see if he is the one for you. If you love someone, set them free. If they come back to you it is meant to be, if they do not, it wasn't meant to be."

That point was familiar.

Mom gave me a strong blessing, and told me to go for it, to go find out about Dad before it's too late.

Spring of 1968

Dad asked, "Where is Ah Lian?"

I could hear the tone of his deep voice break past my tiny sobs. Nobody answered. Nobody knew.

The taxi was waiting on Dad. It was to take him from our house in Kluang to Singapore, where he would fly off to Indonesia.

Dad bade farewell to Mom first. She was the strongest. She didn't even cry. Then he hugged my sisters and brothers. The taxi driver was loading his luggage into the truck. That's when I ran.

"Ah Lian!" Dad called again.

They all started calling my name. "Ah Lian! Where are you? Ah Lian, where are you?" Again and again, everyone yelled for me.

Dad found me in his bedroom closet. I had told myself if I didn't come out, this would all go away like a bad dream. But there he was, looking down on me, in his traveling clothes. He bent down, scooped me up, and carried me outside. All the while I was in his arms he kept saying that everything would be fine. "You be good and stay with your mom and sisters and brothers. They need you. Mother needs you, Ah Lian. She needs you to help now, to be a big girl in the house." He told me not to cry again.

I said okay, that I would stop. I nodded repeatedly. Yet, the tears kept rolling down my baby face. I felt so sad. I did not want to let him go. Dad was leaving us for a foreign country, Indonesia, and it was very far away.

How am I going to see Dad?

Suddenly he will be gone. Tomorrow there will be no Dad in our home. Our lives, for the first time, will be without him. Tears rolled out my eyes, out of control, saturating my dress. It felt like it would never dry, there were so many tears piling up in the same spot.

We reached the taxi. Of course, Mom and my sisters came to my side, holding my soft little hands, consoling me and begging me not to cry. I could see that their eyes were red too. Even Mom's eyes were red. What do you know? . . .She was just like me.

Then life was hard.

Yet, as days turned into weeks, months and then years, we became used to it. We learned to live without his presence in the home. His energy was there, supporting us. He sent money always, for school, food, everything, for all nine. Money was always coming by mail. The idea of Dad never went away.

He would return once a year for the Chinese New Year. That's what we ultimately got used to—seeing Dad once a year. Boy, was that a busy time. Looking back, I don't know how Dad survived it.

He'd be home for one week. Visitors, family, anyone who ever met Dad would be hopping in and out. The guests were constant, like all the noise from conversations. The house would be so busy and filled with masculine energy.

Every day he was home, as soon as the first beam of sun came through the east window, Dad would scream everyone's names. "Mun Yung! Sow Keng! Pau Chu! Ah Lian!" It was time to shower and clean up. He didn't care if it was a school day, a holiday, a religious day, he hated lazy people and he wanted his children up, up, up. Being well groomed was top priority. And smelling good, that was up there on the list, too.

Lots and lots of goodies came home with Dad: mandarin oranges, apple, grapes, all sorts of sodas and other Indonesian snacks like shrimp and *keropok*. He always had something shiny for Mom, like a gold pendant or a ring, or colorful semiprecious stones. For us there were new clothes, so that we'd look special for the holiday. Sometimes, he'd have beautiful fabrics in colors that reminded us of the land we had never seen; they'd be fuchsia and emerald. He brought those for Mom, too. On the eve of the Chinese New Year, his third night home, he'd sneak into our rooms and put those red envelopes under our pillows. Money! We had a bit of money for our futures. "Oh, thank you, Daddy," I would whisper to myself the next morning.

The next line of business after gifts were passed around was a walk to the local grocery store. Dad had to settle up with the owner, Chen Ann. He had usually loaned us two to three months' worth of food by the time the holidays came around. He said he was happy to do it. He and Dad would shake and bow, and both would say, "Thank you very much" to the other. Dad thanked him the final time for taking care of his whole family. Dad was very grateful there was a man to watch over us, even if the grocery store owner was just looking out for our bellies.

Dad left the family to make more money. Logging in Indonesia doubled his income most of the time. During the rainy season, it's dangerous for vehicles to operate at a logging campsite. So if it rained, it meant Dad couldn't work. When it rained for a season every year, we didn't get any help financially for months. That responsibility fell on Mom's shoulders. Can you imagine having to provide resources to feed nine kids, to pay school fees, bus fares, a mortgage on the house and motorcycle, and medical bills? That's the kind of worry only Mom and the Almighty know about.

I have a secret to share. Of course, being the youngest and standing beside her for nineteen years, I watched her intently as she managed the family. I was a wee observer, like a fly on the wall, as they say. I watched the happiness, sadness, and madness erupt and settle under our roof. I had front row seats for a show that was called My Mother's Beautiful Life. I've never had to manage under the circumstances that she did. I swear, I could write another book on it. (That's my secret.)

Living in the Indonesian jungle meant being in touch was by telegram. The telegrams would come sporadically and they'd be in Bahasa Indonesia or English. Jenny or Debbie or my uncle would have to translate for Mom. Hearing from the Kluang Postal Service was normally a delight, as these telegrams meant that Dad would be in Singapore. In Singapore, Dad was able to phone home. We'd go crazy waiting for that day. We'd gather like geese at the door and walk about 3 miles in a straight row down the road to the public telephone booth. Watching that phone in silence, waiting for it to ring so we could all have one minute with Dad, was torture. All the anticipation ended in relief and satisfaction, of course, as Dad never failed to call. Except, afterwards, we'd walk back home in silence. And I'd be trailing behind like a sad little duckling. It just wasn't enough.

A telegram came in 1974. That one wasn't about gathering around the public phone booth to get a minute with Dad. This one, when translated, said Dad wanted Mom to travel to Singapore to meet him for a two-night stay.

A few years went by after that. Then one day a telegram requested Mom's presence in Indonesia for an extended stay. She was gone for three months. We were bigger then, so we managed. Two years after that, Dad wrote her to come again. Mom left for eight months. Pau Chu was in charge. She knew Mom's duties by heart by then. She basically replaced her, caring for Richard, Jason, Charles, and myself. The girls all cared for themselves, but I was a bit young to have all the control. Even though Pau Chu could do everything that Mom did, and just as efficiently, it wasn't the same. Mom's absence cut to the core, especially at night. Is it me, or can life get a little bit lonelier after the sun goes down? I missed her so much. Our food didn't even taste right without her magic touch. No word can express the loneliness that hung heavy like mist after an afternoon rain shower.

During the Chinese New Year, when Dad was around, it meant Grandmother and all the aunties and uncles were there, too. We made the grandest of dinners. Mom cooked for days. All the girls cleaned. It was open house at the Tham residence. We took in all the neighbors—Christian, Muslims, Indian, Sikhs, Chinese. We had so many friends. They all wanted to see Dad. Who could blame them? Mom always made sure no one left our house without a full belly. She'd make beef hive, biscuits, dishes with peanuts, sunflower seeds, and *kueh belandah*—Chinese love letters for dessert. Those were pastries rolled and baked and etched with symbolism. You could sneak a note inside them if you wanted. We'd have all those special sodas from Dad in green and orange and purple, and, of course, tea and powdered coffee. We also traveled to our neighbors' places for their New Year celebrations and special dates, and dined on their families' traditional cuisine. Sharing was big. The Chinese New Year for us was extra special, though, as it was the only week we'd have with Dad before returning to his camp and the logging company for another three hundred and fifty-some days.

Even though we all adjusted, the challenges of Dad being gone remained the same. Mom had to be both parents. She became the yin and the yang energy in our family. It exhausted her; I could tell. Dealing with Jenny running away and with her bipolar disorder would have been easier with Dad around. At least that's what we all thought. We imagined her disease blowing away in the wind if only Dad were home to fix it. Surely, this was just a bunch of silly dreaming. Nothing can take away her illness, not any drugs, certainly not a strong wind. Mothers and fathers have different strengths. Mom was in charge of our mental, social, and spiritual well-being. The boys in the family didn't have to work like the girls, but Dad was a very hard worker. Back when he lived with us, he was well-respected because of that. He was revered as the first man who went far away to Never Never Land to seek better resources to support his family in Kluang. We, his children, have always been so proud. On the other hand, there was no longer a man to admire or look up to every day. Mom was lonely, and sometimes she was angry. We could tell. We gave her room to breathe in both cases. Mom had to go to every social event alone now that Dad was logging. There wasn't a man to hold her hand, or tell her she looked pretty before she left the house, or even look at her with that smile that a husband shares only with his wife. She went everywhere alone, like a widow. Except she wasn't a widow. Even widows were free. Mom had someone in a far off place, in Never Never Land, that she had to ultimately answer to. Even if Dad didn't know everything about our lives, or her life, which he didn't anymore, Mom did. Mom knew everything, and she saw everything. She was there. She knew her role. She had deep faith and values. She knew the rules in her heart, and she followed them to a T. And when she wasn't thinking about the rules, it was because she was working from dawn until dusk. She worked through sicknesses and sadness. She was worried all the time about food for her children. This is why so much of her jewelry (gifts from Dad) didn't last more than a few months before it found a new home in the pawnshop. *"The prettiest gold ring in the world isn't worth keeping once you've heard the rumble of your child's belly, Ah Lian. One day, you too, will understand."* She'd say before parting with her latest token of Dad's love....

I did understand, for I could hear her belly, too, sometimes at night. But I didn't dare say that. Mother never once talked about her own hunger. And I respected that.

c h a p t e r n i n e

People with the lucky number nine are endowed with the gift to serve others.

The Morning of June 1, 1987

WE WERE AT SUBANG Airport, in Kuala Lumpar, Peter and I. It was before Kuala Lumpar International was built. We held each other tight. Boy was it a mad house. Over his shoulder and through eyes blurry with tears, it became apparent I wasn't the only person going on a journey. Maybe June was the month to travel…? This was back when your fathers, mothers, brothers, sisters, and lovers got to escort you practically onto the plane. I miss that, now that I think about it. I miss watching strangers hug and kiss and give blessings to those they love before departing. There was unity in that, in seeing other people say goodbye. I kissed Peter, and then bent down and grabbed my bag. I had but one bag (that was mostly filled with anxiety), and off I went to Borneo, Indonesia to spend time with my father.

The trip getting into the village should have told me everything I needed about the place. I flew to a small town called Tawau, Sabah, which was still in Malaysia, and spent the night there. The next morning, I left for the Tawau airport again, but this time I got on an eight-seater. Once they fired up the engine, that tiny plane vibrated so hard from the propeller spinning, my nose itched nonstop as we glided down the tarmac to cue up for takeoff. I was happy, nervous, scared, and prayed that seeing Dad would go well. I had to look way up and out my window to see the tops of the coconut trees. It was like I was in a car; that's how low to the ground I felt. The engine was so loud it buried most of my fear. I landed in Tarakan, east of Kalimantan, Indonesia an hour or two later, and then hopped on a transit. I waited two hours in transit there, then took off again for two more hours to the Berau Airport. This got me into the general area. Here, I could see the villagers cropping by the river as we landed. The whole world had turned green. Dad was waiting for me. I was a little girl in his eyes again—that sensation overwhelmed me.

A local taxi took us through town, which was filled with goats, cows, chickens running all over, and a ton more coconut trees. A family with children—three or four—flew past us on a motorbike. They waved and smiled big. No one was wearing a helmet. Fruit sellers on bicycles moved from one spot to another. They kept stopping to sell from their balancing baskets. The fruit must have been amazing. It seemed like they were getting nowhere fast. I call that good business. We had a late lunch in a hut. It was made by a lady who was selling local specialties, like rice wrapped in coconut leaves with peanut and turmeric, sweet and sour sauce, and fresh chilies. It was very delicious. During my breaks from working with Dad, when I was in the city, I would have lunch here regularly.

Early Evening, June 2, 1987

From Berau, we got in a long, motorized boat with eight or nine too many people (in my estimation), including children, pregnant ladies, folks who were very old—eighty years or more—and women with new babies, too. This was a two-and-a-half hour-long adventure to get to Dad's logging camp. As we traveled, we watched villagers shower on the river, wash their clothes, get their water in containers for the next day. Kids swam on the riverbank. Also, all the toilets were built on the water's edge. They were squatting right there, making it easy to eliminate waste directly into the river, as they did not have septic tanks. Immediately, I felt these people were somehow lucky to live with such freedom.

Everything flowed into the river mouth. There were branches and giant logs from old dead trees floating at us as we sailed onward. The motorist knew instinctively how to maneuver around them to avoid a collision every time. This was the only mode of transportation to and from the logging camp. It was a hot and shaky trip. I was floating away from civilization. Berau was where all our modern-day needs were: groceries, banking, Chinese/Indonesian clothing stores, and other shops. It was looking smaller and smaller by the minute. And I didn't ask, probably because I didn't want the answer, but there wasn't a single life jacket in sight. Honestly, this little boat scared the shee— out of me. Another five inches and we were sure to sink.

But we didn't.

Sink.

I didn't sink.

There was a jungle there, too, at Dad's camp: Tanjung Redep. From a distance, it looked just like the one from my childhood back at Lambak Estate 1. It didn't look the same close up, but welcomed me with open arms just the same.

My first dinner was a series of specialty dishes per Dad's instructions. This put me at ease right off the bat.

The first routine I got into was jogging. I'd rise at 5:00 a.m. It was true freedom entering the jungle every morning like I used to do as a girl. I had running, like in high school. I had the wet earth beneath my feet, and the green jungle as a backdrop.

One day, while on my routine in the lodging camp, I stumbled upon a mudpuppy named Milo. He was five months old. I trained him to walk and jog with me. I adopted him! He'd react to a special whistle. When I made the sound, he'd jump and find me, and off we went—the buddy system. Having Milo as company put Father at ease.

But the wild boars were braver and bigger in Borneo, and they chased me anyway. I'd have to jump into a tree. I'd be humming a song, or singing under my breath in Bahasa Malaysian; "Kerana" by the Alleycats was a favorite of mine. *"Kerana kau ku masih di sini, Kerana kau ku bisa menangis"* (I had outgrown the *Saturday Night Fever* Soundtrack). Then in a flash, I'd be leaping into a tree, a wild boar snapping at my heels. Fortunately, I was still fast, and retained my leaping skills from long jump. Huge snakes slid onto my path, crawling out from their nests, stretching to ready themselves for a new day like me. They freaked me out at first, too. Just as the boars were faster and wilder, the millipedes were larger and more vibrant. In wonderful shades of orange, twelve inches long and fat, the millipedes would creep along my jogging trail. I'd collect them inside my pocket and bring them to my office. I had a tree in a pot there, with tentacle-like branches. They'd wrap about them and stretch and crawl as I'd watch in fascination. The snakes were bigger than any I'd ever seen. I guess that stands to reason. They seemed friendly enough, though, once we both got used to each other. And, of course, it was warm and misty like the jungle back home. That part was the same. Running cleared my head and prepared me for a new day with Dad in my life. Also, I had my best friend and jogging partner, Milo, for comfort.

Immediately, I felt the change from city to simple living. As soon as the light peeked in through my bedroom window, my eyes would pop open. I'd jump up to catch the sun rising to greet the village. You could always count on the sun. My eyes went wide and round like big white moons, like they were challenging this god of heat and light: *I can do that, too. I can be big and bright like you.* The world looked crystal clear from my campsite window. Peace had finally united with the marrow in my bones. It was a part of me now. This reaction was immediate. It was the village, though, not anything my Dad had done.

The local people were primitive. For starters, they were all barefooted, walking miles upon miles to work, and then home again. Over time, we'd see less and less of each other, as they had to go deeper into the jungle to create new rice crops every season. Nonetheless, I looked forward to being greeted by the villagers in the same way, just like my morning prayers and mantra got me revved for the day. They walked and worked while carrying their babies inside a handmade basket on their backs. They all had perfect posture from those babies, but that's not why they were strapped to their backs. It was because their hands were occupied with the knitted baskets and mats that held home cooked lunch and black tea. The baskets they carried were filled with all sorts of things they needed to transport to work and for everyday living. The babies stayed with them all day while they cropped. This was jaw dropping—seeing people living their lives without shoes and doing their jobs with their babies along for the ride. And the babies—none of them were ever crying. They were all smiling, and they'd wave to me like I was their grand mamma or someone extra special like that.

The villagers said good morning in a dialect I couldn't understand, just like the croppers in the rice fields. I didn't speak their language and they knew it, yet they all said hello, good morning, and good night anyway. I saw them use sign language frequently, with me and among themselves. That's when I realized that we're all not so different. Language is just one way to communicate, but we (the villagers and myself) were doing a pretty decent job without it.

During cropping season when the sunset came around, some villagers would spend overnights in the field at their work studios. I called these studios A frame huts. These huts were encircled by strings of empty cans. They'd rattle these cans in the middle of the night if they suspected animals or wild pigs were stealing their crops. I was honored to be invited on a few occasions to have tea with sugar and biscuits and enjoy the sunset with them from the A framed huts. That's how I learned about the simple way to start a fire with some small branches and dry leaves. They'd go to the trouble of lighting a fire to boil water for tea. That was joy for me. We enjoyed eye contact, and signed about how wonderful the weather was. Each time I departed they stood at the entryway and watched me go down the steps, and we'd wave goodbye so hard, like I was leaving for good. In our hearts we felt love and a real friendship. We were neighbors in a previous life, maybe that was it. It was easy to smile, thank God, and count my blessings in Borneo.

I sat on my favorite rock one morning pondering my new life. I had only been there two months at most and already had so much— friendships, afternoon tea parties, a favorite rock! I had heard enough about meditating to know a little bit about how it was done. I breathed in, quieted my mind, took in the energy from the core of the village. It was cold energy because the mornings were crisp, but it enveloped me warmly like Mother's arms. I breathed in the fresh air.

It filled my lungs to capacity. A beam of sunlight shot down from the clear blue sky and warmed my cheeks. I felt that beam melt into my skin and swim down into my body. I could feel the power of our heavenly Father, and the divine power of Mother's unconditional love. My soul grew bigger than it had ever been before. I always thought my body housed my soul, but that morning it seemed like the opposite was happening: my soul was outside my body, surrounding it, protecting it, wrapping it in love. I've never been able to find all the right words to describe that experience, not in Chinese or in English. It was such a precious moment, and so pure. Then I felt a tickle on my cheek. *Must be a moth,* I thought. I went to give it a friendly swat only to discover that it wasn't a tiny fluttering bug saying good morning. My face was covered in tears. I was crying. After a long jog in the cool, dry jungle (for it wasn't the rainy season quite yet), I was overcome by my new world. I was overjoyed. And tears were streaming down my face without my conscious awareness. That was the first time the notion struck me: I am one with God. As soon as I realized what was happening, I made a point to engrave that moment into the book of memories in my mind. And then I dog-eared that page so I could retrieve it at will. I was wholly present. I was happy, strong, aware, perfect, warm, one with the sun and my favorite rock. I even felt a special unity with Milo. I was where I was supposed to be. One with God. One with the universe.

I was the universe.

I was.

I am....

It didn't take much for me to fit in. This is something I hadn't noticed growing up, but I seemed to possess the ability to adapt easily to new environments. It's a talent that I never saw as such, but something I've grown grateful for.

Father was the leader of this camp. It was a very basic environment. The whole camp was operated by a single generator. Most nights after work, Dad would sit down to unwind. We enjoyed black tea served by Marthina. Father never forgot to puff from his favorite cigarettes, *Gudang Garam*. "Shrimp salt" is the direct translation from Indonesian for the name of those things. You can imagine how they smelled; pungent was putting it mildly. We wouldn't relax for long though, as Dad always thought of something. He'd generally instruct me to summon, one by one, the managers from different departments for a meeting. He needed to find out what the loggers faced in the jungle that day, and what parts were low in the workshops. Discussing which heavy vehicles broke down in the jungle was always an intense topic. Also, we had our own canteen. It was Dad's job to buy all the supplies every two months. We managed our canteen, and sold knick-knacks and supplies to our employees as they needed them. Everyone couldn't be going into town all the time.

I worked for Dad and one of his assistants. I called him Uncle: *Pak Salim* in Bahasa Indonesian. He was a Hakka Chinese man. With a patient disposition, Pak Salim taught me how to measure logs, make calculations for productions, how to calculate salaries, deduct canteen bills, and give loans to employees accordingly.

Dad was a caring man. He had 200 employees under his supervision; he knew every one of them well. He built a long house for the bachelor division on the foothill of the campsite and provided several cooks for them. The cooks were responsible for cleaning and laundry too. He built another separate long house for the couples and families who had kids. He did not provide them with a cook, but compensated with more money, as their wives took care of shopping, cleaning, and cooking. But our management's long house—that was the best. Dad had built that on top of the hill. It was overlooking the river mouth that dipped into the sea, which you could see far away with just a glance. It was magical. The jungle surrounded it. The air was so clean and fresh. It was important to be close to the river mouth, our main source of water. This was also where we spent most of the time in the morning and evening sitting on the floating logs, watching the sun rise and set. We fished and caught prawns there, too. This was where that small motorboat was docked. (You know the one without the life jackets—that one that was the only form of water transportation from our campsite to downtown Berau). That two+ hour trip was taken once a week by the housekeeper in order to stock up on groceries, food, kitchen and cleaning supplies. We were lucky to be able to test all the organic local produce like fresh tempeh, fermented soy, *paku pakis*, wild jungle fern, tofu, salted fish, *jengkol*, salted egg, dry noodles, and meat and chicken.

I stayed with Dad at the long house. This is where I learned about his love of plants. Dad had a whole bunch of them he manicured and watered daily. He spoke to them, too. I'd watch from the door as he'd whisper secrets and compliment them on their rich colors and full leaves, or for sprouting a new bud. They were perennial canna lily plants with tropical foliage. They required a lot of water and sunlight. Dad grew them in red, orange, and yellow. Their leaves could be used in cooking; they'd be wrapped around fish or wild boar and give off a special aroma. Dad also kept two sets of rabbits, and he fed them scraps of greens from the kitchen every morning. It was sweet and surprising to see the feminine side of Dad. Who knew? Certainly not me.

Dad was very protective while I was there. It was like I was a girl again, but one who had a dad. He reminded me to be extra careful on my early morning runs. He never allowed me to swim at the river mouth, as one of the workers was bitten by a crocodile. That man lost his left leg. It wasn't good. So this is what fathers did when they weren't working, scolding, eating, or sleeping—they taught their daughters how to protect themselves.

I was also in charge of accounting and the general welfare of all employees. The city had trained me well for this job, no problems there. I was so happy because every day we made a plan to have breakfast, lunch, and dinner together, alone and with other colleagues in the long house kitchen. Our food was slightly more delicious because special items and expensive ingredients were purchased to feed Dad's team. Log buyers and special guests from Jakarta or Holland would join. Compared to the budget given to the bachelor and families' kitchens, we ate like royalty.

I felt so lucky to be with both my dad and Mother Nature.

One of the biggest and most unforgettable moments was a special world sports day. The employees and I requested Dad only work two hours so that we could watch Mike Tyson vs. Michael Spinks. This was on June 27, 1988. This was the final fight. It had brought in the most money in boxing history to date. We wanted Dad to forgo one day of work. That meant no production in the jungle or workshop, and the whole camp would be on a holiday celebration. It meant the whole camp would be invited too. Everyone from babies to seventy- and eighty-year-old grandpaps were welcome to huddle up around the management's big TV theater system to watch the final boxing match of Tyson and Spinks. Dad said yes to it all! What a day! Plus, the boxer we were rooting for, Tyson, took down Spinks in ninety-one seconds. A knockout! These people lead very secluded lives. This celebration was as good as being at the live match. It was incredible. "Soda drinks all around from our canteen," Dad instructed. He was so happy about the win, he even announced, "Wild boar on the house, too!" All the cooks and wives gathered in the main kitchen and cooked a big, sumptuous dinner for the whole camp.

———— ◆ ————

I thought I knew Dad, but the image in my mind was quite off. His girlfriend, Marthina, was even more of a surprise. I wanted to dislike her, but how could I? I was raised to believe people did their best. If being the mistress to my father was her best self, I had to accept that, and thank the heavens that she wasn't any worse. *Maybe sharing a bed with my father kept her from robbing banks. . . .* I had to believe there were worse crimes, so that I could get to know my father without judgment.

Marthina took care of all matters in the long house, from groceries, cooking, and washing to cleaning. It was impressive. As days, weeks, months and a year went by, we became friends. I asked her what had happened regarding the fight with my mom. (This had been debated on many an occasion back home.) She confessed to loving my dad for years. She was the one who cared for him when he was sick and missed home. She's been there to comfort and accompany Dad through terrible times. She only ever asked for friendship in return, and they gave each other unconditional love. "Was it wrong?" she asked me one day. I didn't have enough life experience to come up with an answer. And she's traveled all these years from one camp to another with Dad—Balikpapan, Surabaya, Samarinda, Berau, and Iran Jaya. She's been loyal to my dad this whole time, and she's also supervised the budget over housekeepers and staffs at all the long houses, too.

Their gypsy kind of love story touched my heart. I broke down and silently accepted her kindnesses. We hugged and cried, too. I kept her friendship and story to myself for a long while, but I thanked her for all she'd done. I don't know how easily Dad would have survived without her. There are two sides to every story.

———— ♦ ————

During the rainy season, our two outstanding employees, Landak and Augustinus, from Sulawesi, became our top two full-time hunters. They hunted wild boars and monkeys like true warriors. They carried chilies and salt in a small bag inside their back pockets. They wore only shorts and no T-shirts went they hunted.

We hunted for our meat, and built fires to cook our dinners. I learned how to spear a wild boar. This was why it was such a big deal when Dad let everyone have wild boar on the house on world sports day. Killing a boar was hard work. It required hunting dogs and poison spears; the only thing missing was the war paint. The wild boars would hide, the dogs would bark and leap, then we would leap, and then the spear would fly in what seemed like slow motion into the throat of the beast. Never did it target the dogs; it would go for the beast like the head of the arrow housed a computer chip that had been programmed to plunge right into their throats. As soon as we got on top of the hill near the long house after a hunt, Landak, Augustinus, and myself checked our bodies for leeches. If we had some, they'd grab a container of tobacco juice, splash it on those fleshy creatures, and they'd slide right off.

That was what life in the jungle was like.

This was normal and common for them, it was habit. For me it took a while to get used to, but eventually I managed. When in Rome.... Then we'd cook up our kill by the fire. The best part was the liver; just like the French gourmet dish, fois gras. Food of gods! It was our special treat of the day, sometimes our treat of the month. We'd enjoy it before we'd carry the wild boar and distribute to the entire long house kitchen accordingly. This tasted nothing like chicken with rice and honey, but I loved it just the same. This hunting adventure would often happen two and three times a week during raining season. It all depended on the weather.

The hunting wasn't just about all the mouths we had to feed. I think there was something special and primal about killing the boars with spears. It was a natural high, a big accomplishment; it took patience and a fast and steady hand. It seemed like an addiction for some of the people. Like my mother with her cigarettes, some of the campers had to get their fix and kill "a boar a day." Endorphins.

Besides hunting, we fished a lot during the rainy season. We cooked fish and prawns on the fire. Catfish was popular with chili and salt. Not only did Landak and Augustinus welcome me on their boar hunting adventures, they taught me how to catch my own fish and prawns in the river and jungle pond. They taught me how to be a survivor. One time, they caught a wild dog and chopped it into, well, minced dog. Then they stuffed it inside a big bamboo shoot and smoked it over the fire. I had never seen that before. The earth mixed with the bamboo trunk, which mixed with the dog meat. It was unbelievable. Another time we cooked chicken by burying it in the ground above a hole that was dug deep in the earth with a fire lit inside. The heat from the earth slow-cooked the chicken. You can imagine how moist the chicken was. This tasted just like chicken with honey and rice, except there was no honey or rice, just the juices from the chicken heated by the earth.

During the hot summers while on lunch break, we'd see a heat of wild boar with eight, nine, ten baby boars crossing from our campsite to the river mouth. Wild boars swim just like dogs in the water. How lucky I felt to see wild boars crossing the street like a mother with her ducklings.

Life was quiet. That part wasn't surprising. I didn't have any solid image of what would happen after my arrival. I went without expectation. (Mother had said that to me, too; she said plan to be surprised.) When you get used to living in the city, it's an interesting process for the mind to adapt to the sounds of the jungle. Silence would be broken by crickets or a howl, but never from the horn of a car, or music from a neighbor's jukebox.

I had planned to stay for two years, but it had been three since I'd heard a door slam, or a tire screech to a halt on a paved road. That occurred to me one day jogging. And I didn't miss that…until the morning when I rose with the sun, strapped on my shoes and my belt that carried my pocket knife for self-defense, hit the soft earth, entered the jungle, and realized that I did miss the city—the lights at night, the colors in the streets by day. I missed the busy open-air street eateries that were ready to serve us at dawn and closed late at night so that all the city folk could enjoy their delicious food. I missed the *nasi lemak* on banana leaves, *mee goreng, kopi-o, chow kueh teow* with *kerang, bak kut teh*. I longed to go dancing and karaoke

119

singing, and to high tea with friends. And I felt desperate to take a three-hour train home to visit my family.

It was time.

———◆———

So, I've written in detail about the jungle, the people, the sights and sounds, fishing and spearing wild boars, and fitting in magically. And I talked about the beautiful babies with friendly smiles. But how was it with Dad...?

In my eyes, Dad was strict and fierce. We were scared of him growing up. We dared not approach him directly about anything— buying shoes, going to a movie, etc. After staying with Dad, I've come to learn he was easy going, and our conversations were nice. Just like he had meetings nightly with his subordinates, we, too, would have our dad-daughter get-togethers prior to "lights out," just to get a feel for each other's day. When the generator was switched off by Augustinus at 21:00 hours, our meetings would come to a close. The blackness that blanketed the campground reminded us to rest in order to prepare for another challenging jungle day in the logging camp.

As the youngest girl in the family, I was taught to never speak up or ask adults direct questions. But here in the jungle, Dad was okay with me asking; it was our way of getting to know each other. I was allowed to ask Dad if he needed my help with anything, too.

I now know for certain that Dad did his best. I saw him rise before the first beam of sunlight, and actually do his best every day. As I came to know life in the jungle, I watched my father lead with an honest and kind, but firm, heart. I finally understood the massive life sacrifice he made for us every day and night living in the jungle with God knows what.

His simple, remote life was to ensure we'd all have big lives outside of the jungle. At the same time, he was proud of his hard work. He invited Mom, Angie, Richard, Charles, Jason, and myself to stay with him at different times. Even though he wanted more for us, he honestly wanted to show us he cared for his children. He knew the only way to do that was to bring us into his world, join him and Mother Nature. That was a risk he took, over and over. Being the patriarch in the family and being vulnerable for each of his children like that can't have been easy for Dad. I know that now.

And so it had been three years. I was a new woman. Defined by new things. I was created from the soul of my mother, but now I was also my father's daughter. I had an additional title. It felt right. I hadn't cooked with a stove, or been in a car in three years. I wasn't in charge of clubs and talent here. I did build a theater. And I set up sports. I started teams and taught badminton and volleyball. We built two courts for both the games. The ground was not quite perfect for those, but the enthusiasm outweighed the wet, sticky soil. People who live this kind of primitive lifestyle are naturally fit; it didn't take much to launch sports teams. Although I didn't know how to play, I brought a soccer ball for them to use, too.

I used my skills from being in charge at the Canossian Convent School and from my promotional work to organize special benefits for the school-aged children on the neighborhood islands. With nothing to distract me, like television, a regular job, or a boyfriend, I was able to turn my focus outward and help. My eyes were so open to the needs of the kids and villagers; it wasn't a matter of what to do next, it was a matter of naturally offering assistance based on my own skill set. Life had fallen into place effortlessly on Borneo Island.

There was an unspoken mutual respect inside the walls of camp. Dad had that when he was at home, our respect. But it was out of fear back then. Here, it was just respect. I was given it, too. Because I was his daughter? I don't know. People were kind to me. Still, when it was time, it was easy to return from this obscure world that felt so much farther away from my other life, a lot farther than 1,400 kilometers (900 miles). It wasn't that I knew my father and I had finally had enough, for that would never be the case with the ones I loved. It was easy to go because that day, on my favorite rock, changed my life. Since then, I learned the voice in my heart is the only voice I need. And it was telling me to move on, go and learn something new....

————•◆•————

This is one of my most treasured tales from my time in Borneo—the story of how Landak's treasure stone saved my life.

Dad took off to Malaysia for Chinese New Year like usual. I organized a camping trip twenty kilos deep in the jungle. I did not ask Dad permission to do this before he left (mainly because I sensed he'd say no). Marthina, Augustinus, Landak and a couple of our Borneo colleagues were "summoned" to join. We brought some ducks and chickens, tied those under a tree. We had a volleyball, a soccer ball, and mats for playing on, plus fishing poles, and a shot gun. You never know.

We found a perfect open space not far from the river. We unloaded, and got ready. We cleaned up the ground and pitched a tent. Beside our campground, the water ran fresh for drinking, bathing, and cleaning fish.

Landak and Augustinus checked out the surrounding area and found two people buried not far from our campsite. Landak told me the bodies were sitting upright with lots of colorful stones and other personal belongings around them, per their ritual. We made silent prayers, letting them know we were just passersby, meant no harm, and were not intruding on their privacy.

We were digging, fishing, running around like kids. Some of us were playing volleyball, some were playing soccer. It felt good to set our inner children free without "the boss" around.

The sun was about to set. Automatically, Landak and Augustinus set up a fire and smoked the campground using the wet grass. It was customary. I was lying down to read my book on the floor mat.

Suddenly, my head became itchy. After a few minutes, it worsened. Then my eyes started swelling up big time. I grabbed my tiger balm ointment, but it didn't help. Marthina didn't know how to help me either. Landak came over and asked me for his trust. He pulled out a stone wrapped in silver foil. It was the size of a grain of rice. He filed the stone into a tiny amount of water, said a prayer and applied it to my head. The itching stopped, the swelling went down, and I wrapped Landak in my arms. I couldn't believe it. He said he thought I might have clashed with a negative spirit in the jungle. Then he said his grandfather from Tatoh Rajah of Sulawesi gave him this stone when he ventured out in the world. His grandfather told him to use it when he was in real trouble, especially jungle trouble. I was so grateful to Landak and his magical stone. What a treasure. What an experience.

This is a special story, which I haven't told very often.

The rest of the trip went on as planned, as if that incident had never happened. We walked through the jungle giving thanks to its beauty—the ferns, other plants, Toucans, butterflies, monkeys, ants. The air was so fresh like the jungle was sprinkled with mint. The moon was so big at night it looked like we were all staring at it through a magnifying glass. This was paradise personified. We paid a visit to the dead after packing up on the last day. We thanked them for sharing their space with us. I will always respect the true spirit of the jungle. Mother Nature is a great and powerful creature.

Life wasn't like a fairy tale in Borneo, but it came close sometimes. And just like the Outback in Australia, or the Amazon River in South America, it wasn't scary, just unexplored. It was a simple life there. Except for Dad—the memories I hold of him are now layered and complex; they're rich and sophisticated memories. I wasn't entirely satisfied with the image of Dad I had carried through my young life and into Kuala Lumpur, and so this was a good thing. It seems like when pieces of a puzzle are missing, the best thing to do is seek them out, and then press them into your picture, your story, if at all possible. People can find a father in a neighbor, or a temple, or in a husband, too, I guess. I'm glad I was able to discover my father in the man who made me. There's nothing quite like the feeling of satisfaction from a job well done or a race completed, and that's what if felt like to know Dad—like I had finished a race. I ran a marathon and medaled; that's how I felt leaving Borneo. I had abandoned my old life to seek out the missing pieces of my puzzle and I found the "master" piece.

There I was, getting lucky again.

"The engineer you say you love will be there waiting for you, Ah Lian." Mother had said. "If it's meant to be, he'll be there. Make your choice. Go. Don't look back."

I made the choice. I didn't look back. We wrote. We missed each other as lovers do. I was gone for three years. That's a long time. I didn't expect him to stay. I hoped, though. It's important to hope.

chapter   ten

People with the lucky number nine can usually realize their dreams as long as they have practical plans combined with real actions.

WHEN I WAS YOUNG, Mother and Grandmother insisted I bring spring onions on the first day of kindergarten. I packed them in my green colored school bag, no questions asked. What sounds like superstition to some, can be a deep part of another person's culture. Garlic and leeks were believed to enhance one's ability to solve calculations. Spring onions were for cleverness. They were also a sign of prosperity, intelligence, and were considered beneficial for longevity of life. "Never bring eggs!" they'd shout while shaking a finger. They'd joke about it, but it was true. Eggs meant I'd end up with all zeros. I wanted 100%, so I packed spring onions. Spring onions, garlic, and leeks are symbols of great importance. Calling upon them right from the beginning, in pre-school or kindergarten, increased the chances of harnessing their special powers. I'm not sure if this makes sense to everyone, but in Chinese culture this tradition has been in place for thousands of years. Imagine something you have known to be true for that long, for forever, really, you'd pack it in your green school bag, too, especially if you knew it could bring you straight As.

———◆———

Three years can be a long time, or it can go by in a flash. In the case of my pining for Peter, I had hoped for three he'd be waiting for me. But he wasn't. He met another woman. He didn't mention that in the letters; they were coming in more slowly, but we hadn't lost touch entirely. He seemed angry when we reunited. I guess he had a right to be. I didn't know he had found someone new, though, and that hurt. I was occupied with jungle life, and getting to know Dad. Because of this, I didn't date at all, and I hung onto the idea that my first love was doing the same. How naïve. I allowed the devastation to work through my bones knowing that was the only way to be cleansed of it. I believed, as Mother had said, that God had a plan. I did not regret going, or staying an extra year with my father. I just needed a little time to heal.

I would have several more relationships after this that weren't meant to last. They would end due to differences in money, aspirations, culture. Sometimes an eldest son and the desire for children created an obstacle. Once I turned thirty and found myself still single, I realized motherhood wasn't the path for me. Sometimes it was lack of chemistry that came out over time. Love was a gamble. My relationship with Peter prepared me for that, and I was thankful.

After him, I no longer relied on hope, but faith to walk me through all my adventures in love.

For my old boss, conversely, three years went by fast. He snapped his fingers. "You're back! This is perfect," he said, like no time had passed. Unlike my first love, he had not replaced me, and was ready to start fresh.

Snap: I was gone.

Snap: I was back at work, living the life of a city dweller once again.

I told my Mr. Tan I wasn't interested in club promotions any-more. Borneo had changed me. Then I mentioned being in the mood for a new challenge. With a spark in his eye, he said, "You came to the right place at the right time." He was developing a string of membership only equestrian clubs and golf courses, and private property resorts for high-end residence. He was doing this all over Malaysia. They would be years in development, and then the clubs would flourish; they'd be rich with activity and members that would magically appear, he assured me.

Snap.

We stood atop a hill, looking into the vast wilderness, miles of meadows, as he spoke of this vision. "Before you know it, Rina, this will be worth hundreds of millions. And thousands of rich and famous people from all over the world will become members of our resorts. Ours. Others—local Malaysians and international business people—will become buyers of the properties. Their dream homes will be realized. We will create them. Golf, horseback riding, and recreational clubs will become favorite pastimes.

Snap.

"Politicians, ministers, sultans, royalty, and movies stars from all over the world will be a part of this grand scheme. We're going to give Malaysia a makeover, Rina. How does that sound? Is that something that would be of interest to you? Do you like this challenge? Does it wake you up?"

He certainly woke me up.

Then he snapped his fingers one last time, and there was an equestrian club—the first in Malaysia. His vision had materialized. We did it. And golf courses and private resorts were popping up everywhere, too, just like he had said.

My boss was a very lucky, intelligent, positive, and forward thinking person. He was also a good friend to the current Prime Minister of Malaysia. And the thing was, Dr. M., our Prime Minister, loved riding horses. He was the first to join the very first club. Dr. M. strongly believed that introducing a new sport to Malaysia would bring adventure and joy to the people of his country. He was right.

Dr. Mahathir bin Mohamad (Jawi: محمد بن محضير;pronounced [maˈhaðɪr bɪn moˈhamad]; born July 10, 1925) was the fourth Prime Minister of Malaysia. He held the post from 1981 to 2003, making him Malaysia's longest-serving Prime Minister. His political career spanned almost forty years.

Malaysia was a place of third world workers who stayed afloat thanks to tin and rubber. We were not a noteworthy country, despite the discovery of rubber some seventy years earlier. Dr. M. and his enthusiasm for life were what catapulted Malaysia into a country of industry and prosperity, into the place to be. Dr. M. put Malaysia on the world map for travel, import, export, and everything to do with business.

My boss not only gave me the opportunity of a lifetime with all these new developments, but we ended up working closely with Dr. M., our Prime Minister. He was a great leader. He was so charismatic, humble, hard working, and it was such an honor to know him personally. I had admired his work prior to leaving for Borneo. I never imagined I'd find myself by his side once I returned to civilization.

My boss, Dr. M., and I spent two years at Bukit Kiara: our first equestrian club. We ate breakfast, lunch, held meetings, and rode horses together. To work closely with these men and listen to their visions for the country was a nonstop education. I couldn't put a price on it.

In 1991, Dr. M. announced a New Economic Policy (NEP) he had developed to make Malaysia the leader of the world over the next thirty years. He called this Vision 2020. In addition to steady economic growth, he wanted to break down all ethnic barriers. Like all leaders, Dr. M. did a lot of things that worked, like liberalizing financial regulations to attract foreign investors. This grew the economy beyond his hopes, and put poverty at an all-time low. He also tried a few things that simply did not work, like his attempts to boost the economy even further with what he called megaprojects.

He brought the Formula One Grand Prix to Sepang. He stood up to sultans and royalty, for no one should be above the law. He surrounded himself with smart people. He had great successes and some failures, too, like any leaders do.

We purchased the horses for Bukit Kiara Equestrian Club from all over the world, and hired expert trainers from England House Society to give lessons. The launch was successful. We sold thousands of memberships immediately. That was my job—selling memberships. I learned about land development. I discovered more about horses—like how to exercise them, change their horseshoes, file their teeth, general grooming, and riding—than I ever imagined. We were the premiere horse tack destination providing the best quality and assortment of products that couldn't be matched anywhere. This came at a price, but people paid. Just spending time with these horses was most enjoyable. And that was the real goal. This wasn't just a prestigious riding school, we wanted everyone to learn all about horses—their personalities and the power of companionship they possessed.

Simultaneously, other projects were well underway. High-end "dreamland" was being groomed for private housing developments. How to pitch a property to a prospective buyer (or buyers) was another one of my new skills. I learned about Feng Shui, and what a vital resource it was to the industry I was in. It was crucial to have a good Feng Shui master. Proper placement of everything from the angle of the main entrance of the equestrian resort, to placement of living room, master bedroom, and front gate was crucial to the sale of these homes. Should the master bedroom and dining room face east or west? There was a lot to think about.

I also took care of everyone that came through the doors. The Sultan of Brunei, Sultans and Sultana, tons of VIPs, Hong Kong stars, everyone you can imagine came through those doors.

We had two hundred stables for rent. The one-of-a-kind equestrian club was buzzing with national and international guests and future buyers. We had horse-riding classes, dressage classes, jumping practices, trail rides. Some horses were for the management's use, but most belonged to the members. We kept care of their horses. They paid a monthly rental fee. The horses came from Argentina, Australia, Arabia, and all over the world. A gorgeous spa with a sauna was built in the recreation center, along with badminton courts, swimming and whirlpools, and, of course, there were Chinese and Malay restaurants and boutiques.

I didn't know anything about horses going into this, now I rode them daily. When I wasn't on a horse, I was in a limousine with tinted windows. I'd be with the VIP's girlfriends, or their guests. I rode four wheelers as part of my job, too. They were often easier to hop on than a horse. The grounds were huge.

The ultra-prestigious (and first) equestrian resort in Malaysia gave way to the second, and the third. Then golf course clubs, and resorts, one after the other, bloomed up all over like white alder. It was all exactly as my bosses had predicted. Surreal is the only word that comes to mind when describing this new adventure. Life had become surreal. The new memberships and monies for land and housing developments flowed in like never before. The Malaysian economy was booming. Everything was selling like hot cakes. Buyers from all over the world were scooping up our properties and market shares at rocket high prices. A monorail was being built. Everything my boss touched turned into great profit; he was so powerful. I had jumped planets; that's how extreme this change was. But, along with money and kings and prime ministers and sultans, came wives, girlfriends, and trouble, too. And artists and international VIPs can be overwhelming. And demanding. I had so many friends by this point. My life was smooth and comfortable. But it's foolish to think that one can get caught up in the moneymaking, without dipping their toes into the other—greed, secrets, chaos, gossip. *Rina, is this the best you can do? Is this it?* Before long, I was asking that of myself. I had taken on a new job: I was the keeper of all secrets, international, scandalous secrets. It was exciting…and outrageous. Everyone was my friend and felt the need to confide. This went on day and night, until I was on gossip overload. Frequently, men brought their wives and children to ride, swim, and enjoy the facilities on the weekends. And on weekdays the same men brought their girlfriends to wine and dine. This was a place to show off their beautiful girlfriends—actresses, models, etc. As for me as an executive, we played along and were nice to all of them.

Where and how do I draw a line?

…It was time to move along.

This was spectacular, but it wasn't me. Life was so bizarre on such a regular basis, that I grew bored with the spectacle of it all, with the superficiality that came with all this money. One too many sunny days, you might say. My sunglasses just weren't strong enough to keep out all the dangerous rays. I was going to go blind, that much was certain. The voice in my head was quite small at this point, for it was suffocating from all the scandalous information that was now stored up there, but I could still hear it. *What is my purpose? What is my purpose?* Surely, my destiny wasn't riding on a horse next to VIPs, their bodyguards, and one of my own....

It can't be.

Despite my challenging hectic work schedule and high and mighty lifestyle that I was questioning more by the day, I still found time after work to train for yearly marathons. The Terengganu Bridge Run was the latest. I, and a couple of colleagues represented our employer as Company of Sports Toto. I've always loved the discipline of training my mind and body for a marathon. It was a great achievement to finish with a better time every year. The focus of training took away lots of stress at work. Plus, I'd grab a little R&R on the east coast of the Perhentian and Kapas Islands to recover. Sweltering beside a coconut tree on a sandy beach next to the turquoise sea was paradise. A few days of doing nothing but swimming and getting some vitamin D while relaxing was just what I needed. It was the life. Then I'd convince myself to go "back again" into the real world, where I couldn't stop working. These yearly marathons cleansed my body from the stress, anxiety, and anger that comes with jobs in client relations.

After just over three years, I told my dear boss it was time again. I had to further my education; that's how I explained it. It was the only way he'd let me go and not offer me more money. Backpacking came to mind, like when I was a girl fresh out of high school. I thought it might toughen me up.

My colleagues agreed with me wholeheartedly. Backpacking it was. They'd resign, too. That's what they said. This was something. Talk about a pickle. My resignation was hitting my boss hard. The man had already hired and lost me once. This was my second escape…and now I was taking prisoners? I didn't know how to get out of this one. I had to think. Their resignations honestly had nothing to do with me. They have their own right to choose. Still….

We decided to keep the backpacking a secret.

Sharon had a relative in Sweden. She said we could housesit and work in a restaurant he owned. That sounded like a good start. As long as Sharon promised to wait a few weeks before resigning, I said I'd do it. She agreed. Wati wanted in on this adventure, too, but she decided to save as much money as she could before joining. It wasn't practical for her to leave for another six months. "Phew," was all I said to that. She could find us. We promised her we'd be waiting with open arms. Then we said, "Sweden, watch out. The Malaysian Charlie's Angels is coming your way!"

Wati never did make it to Sweden; instead, she went straight to America. Life is stored with lots of surprises. Of course, all of us went and sought out our dreams. We encountered lots of ups and downs. And yet today, Wati is married with two handsome boys. In fact, we're both happily married and reside in Los Angeles. Sharon found her forever man and is happily married, too, and lives in Salt Lake City. I've looked back and wondered if I hadn't mentioned the backpacking, would they have landed in the US? In Malaysia? Would they be married? Single? Would we have stayed in touch? I'm glad the Malaysian Charlie's Angels is still together; it was our fate to have our happy endings in the USA.

We ventured far to discover our own American dreams...and we found them.

————— ♦ —————

So, with spring onions and a change of clothing in my backpack, I left on my own, in the fall of 1993, from Asia to Sweden. I took the first Aeroflot flight they had out from Kuala Lumpur to Sweden. This was a shoestring budget trip. Aeroflot was created back in the 1920s. It was a Soviet Airlines originally, and unique in that it didn't just fly passengers but transported goods, and responded to other tasks as well. Aeroflot had an anti-forest fire patrol. It provided medical transportation services. At one point it was the world's largest airline. Mostly, it was the world's cheapest airline, and easy to hop on in a pinch. The one I took was an ex-fighter plane.

I spent a night in transit in Moscow. My first night gone and I already met a handful of wonderful strangers who allowed me to join them for coffee. The coffee, however, cost me about three American dollars. And it was a tiny cup, like for espresso. I couldn't believe it. Already, I was worried. The journey to cleanse my soul and make straight As in the game of life started with a $3.00 cup of coffee.

You must have a reason for me....

I first searched for this reason while house sitting in Sweden (I actually babysat there, too). I also worked as a housekeeper, and a waitress for special functions like weddings or private venues at her relative's restaurant. But Sweden was cold and dark. It looked like midnight when it was noon. Sharon finally joined me, which was a relief, and off we went on a Viking boat to Norway and Finland. Then we visited friends of mine, Judy and Ronnie, in Berlin. They hosted us and served as tour guides for two weeks. That was fun, but also very cold. It was beautiful to visit all the old museums and churches in every country. I was fascinated with the history of churches and temples of all types. The sky was the limit. Where do I start? Where do I go next?

———◆———

...However, people with the lucky number nine are likely to boast a surplus of success with limited real action...so they must be careful what they wish for....

———◆———

137

Dad was home with Mom by that time. He had retired. I'd seen them both before my departure. It was so strange to see him in the home when it wasn't the Chinese New Year. It wasn't turning out as planned, though, his retirement. Something was wrong with Dad, and no one knew what. He was restless. Maybe being home after a twenty-year absence was too much. Was it boredom? Was he cursed? That crossed our minds. Mom considered her karma as the culprit. Maybe that's why Dad was different now, off, unpredictable. I hoped it wasn't that. In any case, there was nothing anyone could do but pray. Mom refused to accept our help. She wanted us off in the world living our lives. She insisted. She was happy to accept monetary help, so my siblings and I sent money when we could. And off I went, as instructed.

After six months, Wati phoned to say the United States was calling her. She had a friend who had housing.

By the following year, Sharon and I had seen most of Europe. She took off to join up with Wati in USA. That's when I went to Hong Kong. Angie convinced me that Charles and she needed assistance with his furniture company. (The main factory was in Indonesia. This allowed Angie time to study at night and during weekends. I would have time to myself, too.) All my searching brought me back to Hong Kong. God knows why. I didn't particularly care for it.

I helped Charles with the furniture at home base (HK), while studying the want ads and the healing powers of *reiki* in my free time.

My reiki teachers were none other than Barbara McGregor and Keven Duff. These gurus (or Master Teachers) were responsible for founding the Usui Reiki Network in 1990, which linked their graduates all over the globe. They had trained over 40,000 practitioners in Australia and all over Europe and Asia by the late 1990s. Their healing philosophy was based on self-help and accountability, which was established by Mikau Usui of Kyoto back in the 1920s.

Reiki is a technique for healing that is Japanese in origin. *rei* means "God's wisdom," and *ki* stands for "life force energy." Reiki means spiritually guided life force energy. It uses energy to heal. If our life force energy is low, that's when we're susceptible to sickness. This practice is used to make a body powerful and whole again. The practitioner's life force energy flows into the patient through the placement of their hands. It's a passive treatment and does not require pressure or movement. This energy (which is transmitted from one being to another) is everywhere, and in all of us. Reiki is intended to heal the mind, body, spirit, and anything with a life force, which includes everything. Considering my dad was losing his mind, and Jenny has had issues her whole life, it was time I learned something that could be of use. Also, I was keeping busy.

One day, after practicing reiki, I was reading the classifieds—through another string of positions I was entirely overqualified for—when I stumbled upon something interesting. "Angie, listen to this one," I yelled. "International Sales Manager. Must be independent, a hard worker, be able to travel throughout Asia, Singapore, Indonesia,

Thailand, Malaysia, and more. Bilingual a must. Serious inquires only."

Angie had had enough. "I told you to go see Nancy. You have nothing better to do. All you do is pray in a corner to no one and make your hands dirty with that newspaper. I will pay for you to see Nancy. She'll tell you. She'll tell you everything you need to know. It's worth it to me, to put my own mind at ease." Angie stood in the entryway of my room with her arms crossed tight.

Sister #4 wasn't referring to an "Aunt Nancy," that's for sure. She was talking about Nancy McCarry, the world famous psychic. She lived in Tennessee, but was visiting Hong Kong. She was one of Princess Diana's psychics. My sister just loved her. Angie said I wasn't going to find my path with my nose in a newspaper, and that Nancy would help.

I made an appointment. It turned out to be the first of many meetings. Nancy McCarry said I was about to fly. Life was about to change drastically, and get hectic, and when it did, I'd better be ready. She called me "the girl in the sky." She saw electrical poles, too, but didn't know what that signified. Then there was a vision. I was a mother for Angie in Mongolia taking care of her in a past life. She told me I would do well financially, and end up in the USA. She asked if I knew why I would be going there.... I had no clue. I had an open mind and was curious about all the things she saw. To me, it all sounded like a fairy tale, but I stored her visions in my memory bank, just in case.

Years later, I met up with Nancy and some others in Macau to cruise the Nile River. We went to Egypt with sixty other healers from all over the world. With special permits we meditated inside the temples at midnight, or on the full moon, or for special celebrations.

My first reading with her was five months before my birthday on March 6, 1995. After that date, she cautioned, *"Your life energy field will take a sharp turn, and the biggest success of your career will materialize."* And that's when she added that I was the girl in the sky. She had said so much, but that's what I held onto from that two-hour session.

I had called on the International Sales Manager position a few days before I met Nancy. After a dozen interviews, the job was mine. After that, I was called in regularly to participate in their sit-in meetings with the company's national and international management team. This was without pay. My mind was so open after my psychic reading, and I was so willing to learn, I thought there was nothing to lose (and nothing better to do in Hong Kong as it were). They'd call, and I'd go join a meeting without notice.

Angie was terrified the whole time. "This is one of those sex rings. They're going to sell you into prostitution! You need to watch it."

"Angie, I'm a thirty-year-old woman."

Then she'd respond, "It's very popular right now, Rina. Prostitution."

I had to do a double take in the mirror, to try and see what Angie saw. "Angie, if I wanted to go into prostitution, I'd just do it. I don't think I'd have to interview ten times to be a prostitute—three or four at the most! Get real!" I mean, I didn't know much about it, but that seemed logical.

On my third day traveling to the Kowloon office of Tsim Sha Tsui, Hong Kong, they officially hired me for actual money. My boss, Tony, called and asked me to join him and the team in China the next day. The HR department would arrange for it. I was off on a one-month internship in the Guangzhou Province in China to learn the ropes. I didn't know what to expect in terms of workload and accommodations. But I reminded myself to be alert, calm down, listen, learn, and relax.

Angie kept on with her suspicions by phone. "It's a trick. I don't trust them, Rina."

"Oh, Angie. You think they're going to train me now? For a month? To be a prostitute? Do you think I'll get a certificate when it's over? Like an accountant? Something for my wall?" Good grief.... Sometimes sisters fought just to fight. That was my reasoning as I unpacked my bag and set up my essentials in my new temporary home.

On May 3, about three weeks into this training, my boss phoned again and told me to pack it up. He needed me by his side at a meeting the very next morning. I was on a plane. Business people around the world referred to him as the Inflatable King. He was the man behind all things inflatable. He also developed properties, rented office buildings and warehouses, and owned a string of glass factories and power plants—more than anyone in the world. Anything he touched turned to gold. They said he had magic hands. And when he wasn't busy selling inflatable things to every retailer from here to the moon, he was building glass-manufacturing companies all over China. He developed properties beyond China, all the way into the US. Rancho Cucamonga: he's the reason the housing development started there. He owned land in Reno, Palos Verdes, Long Beach. He was a major developer in countless big cities all over the world.

The Inflatable King traveled with an entourage of ten to twenty at all times. I was his right hand person, his number one. I was in charge of everything a personal assistant is in charge of, which was to say—everything. And, I was also took care of all business people traveling with him.

Overwhelming doesn't begin to describe my new life. He was a perfectionist. The pressure was so great that after a year or so, I forgot about things like eating, except for survival. I'm not joking. I lost so much weight that Mother kept insisting I quit before I fade to dust. She said, not only had I lost too much weight, but even worse, I had lost my smile. Mother said that was the part that worried her most.

I think jetlag was part of it, too, in all fairness.

It's true. I wasn't smiling. Crying had become an integral part of my super successful career. He had a little temper, the Inflatable King. It came out daily. It wasn't personal; I was just the first person he'd see in the morning, even before coffee, and the last one at night. I was his dream catcher. Native Americans believe that the night air is filled with dreams, both good and bad. The dream catcher, when hung over or near your bed, swings freely, catching dreams as they float by. The good dreams know how to pass through the dream catcher, slipping through the outer holes and sliding down the soft feathers so gently the sleeper doesn't know that he or she is dreaming. The bad dreams get tangled in the dream catcher, and perish with the light of the new day. I was the net that caught the Inflatable King's bad dreams. It was my job to make sure they disappeared by tomorrow's sunrise. It was a massive undertaking.

The Inflatable King didn't drink or smoke, or gamble, and he didn't have time for socializing. He was a hard working, brilliant businessman. He was the best. If we were traveling with fifteen international guests, it was my job to check everyone in at the airport—find them the best seats, keep everyone calm and content. Even getting through ten or fifteen or twenty names in Chinese and translating them from English to Mandarin, or vice versa, was a nightmare. Remember in Chinese the last name is first, but in English it's not like that. Also, in Chinese the first name and last name look the same to people. Smith or Brown or Gafari, well that was easy, but it's nearly impossible to know if *Ooi* or *Thu* is the first or last name of a client. This caused endless stress at the check-in counter. I cried all day, every day, and openly in front of my guests, my boss, my colleagues, VIPs, innocent bystanders. My tears weren't particular either. But I made more money than I ever imagined possible. More than I dreamt of as a girl, more than at the equestrian club. I learned in triple time about the real business world. It was a crash course. Taking care of the mailroom, taking down minutes, filing, assisting with designs, implementing business practices, client relations, handling stress and the pressure of deadlines and dealing with people, mastering time management, improving communication and team-work with my colleagues all over the world—I had to learn it all.

I experienced my first Hong Kong auction at Sotheby's with the Inflatable King. I sat by his side in awe as he bid on art for his personal collection. Closing a deal to build a power plant in China, closing a deal to build another glass factory, closing a deal for huge amounts of land and a port in Xiamen—these are things I witnessed. Meetings with the mayor. China's Prime Minister came to visit our factory in Fuquing; we escorted him through. The Chairmen of the boards of Bank of America and Wells Fargo, and the chief architect for LAX visited our factories in China. I tried to enjoy moments like those. I worked hard to bury my daily fears of this job and the man I worked for to enjoy those moments. Life was so big. I had graduated from the University of Life and was obtaining my PhD at the University of the World. But it was hard to enjoy each moment as they flew by so fast.

And then Debbie called.

...And life was suddenly small again.

I could barely remember the last three years. *Had I been up in the air with the Inflatable King for that long?* Yes, I had. I went home for the Chinese New Year each winter; that's the only time I had seen my parents. I made a point of saying goodbye each time, because Dad wasn't getting any better.

At least I think I did....

Soldiers of Terracotta sculptures were buried for a thousand years beneath the ground of an art museum owned by the government of the Republic of China. I watched my boss win this collection as the highest bidder at Sotheby's.

It was sensational to witness.

But it didn't mean much anymore.

Debbie had called.

My dad was dead.

chapter eleven

People with the lucky number nine are very considerate in taking care of people who are in immediate need of help.

I LEFT ON A flight immediately.

A quiet chaos comes with death. I arrived home two days later by cab.

Upon arrival, I found myself sitting next to Mom while we purchased the plot where Dad was to be buried. We listened to the director of the funeral home as he explained in detail all the ins and outs of planning a "celebration of life." My sisters Angie and Pau Chu, and brother, Jason, were there too. The only real death I'd ever seen was when I was in Borneo.

It was so different for us here in the civilized jungles of Kluang. Difficult. Tedious. Expensive. Awkward. Painful. Peculiar.

We listened carefully as the director talked of the different plots, price differentials, various locations, group plots, and other "amenities" from which to choose. Then he spoke of coffins—wood ones, metal ones, green ones, black ones. Some had brass, some were shinier—14 karat gold plated; their insides were lined in silk, but all pastel in color because that was soothing. Some had pockets. You can bury your loved one with a trinket, a necklace, a ring, a figurine. *Will Father rest better if his dead body is on pink silk as opposed to lilac?* How does one make such decisions. I didn't even know what to say.

Mother did. As soon as there was a break in the director's speech, a chance for us all to think, Mother turned toward me. "I spent my life taking care of that man, Ah Lian." She locked eyes with mine. "I'd gladly do it again; for it was my destiny. But I will not spend the afterlife with him. Do not buy a plot for me next to his grave. My duties stop at death. We buy one plot, for him. After all, I'm only human." She reiterated.

Mother couldn't raise one eyebrow—like people do for effect—but if she had possessed that talent, one of them would have been raised that day as she silenced the room with that statement. I loved my father, but I understood her very well. Of course, she was my mother.

That was 1997. *I spent my life with that man; I will not spend my death with him too.*

Yes, Mother.

———— ◆ ————

I had to kneel all the way from the gate of the funeral grounds to Dad's coffin. It was about fifty yards. It was Chinese culture to give respect, pray with jasmine joysticks in the presence of family members and guests. I looked into his angelic face through the glass coffin, to say goodbye. He would be united with his mother soon. Tears gushed from my eyes. Our time in Borneo was so sweet and special, and it was over, too. Time with my father had come to a close.

My father's death served as a grand symbol or pronouncement that it was time to move on. I flew back to Hong Kong and gave my boss, the Inflatable King, my resignation. If you live with your heart open, fear becomes an adventure; at least that's what I kept telling myself on the flight back. I was a little bit afraid of his reaction, but then I remembered the day he officially hired me. He asked, "What is the most important thing in the world to you?"

I answered that I was born with a hunger to learn, but it was my family above all.

For the next three years, my only breaks from being his personal assistant were to travel back home for the Chinese New Year. This, he understood. Family. And he understood when I gave my resignation. I don't know what I had been so concerned about. Surely I had shed as many tears over my arm. Except with him, I cried openly, on the job. It was typical. The tears didn't wait for bathroom stalls or a cool dry pillow or the dark of the night. They flowed freely all day long and discriminated against no one. I was a real mess; that much I knew. I had a fever and then the shivers. Maybe I was planning on crying, and was more shocked that my eyes had stayed dry. Even tears get tired; that's what I realized the day I left work to spend time with my mother. This part was over. My boss must have known it too. He instinctually felt it as I entered the room; he felt me leaving. He didn't fight it. One of the most successful and richest business-men in the world wished me well, and said he hoped one day I would come back to assist him. I thanked him with all my heart, and with a gentle smile, too. We both knew I wouldn't be back, but it was the respectful thing to do.

Even tears get tired.

Mom had come to Hong Kong with me. If anyone needed a break it was she. Taking care of someone with Alzheimer's was harder than tapping rubber trees day in and day out. Maybe it was just like tapping rubber trees. I hadn't spent enough time at either task to judge. The one thing I could say about rubber trees is if you tap them right, you get results. The same doesn't go for Alzheimer's.

I would call home. Dad would answer, then put down the phone and never let Mom know I was on the other end. He knew how to answer it; he didn't know how to take the steps that followed and call someone else to say hello. Just a year earlier, we were sharing sunrises and smiles; I meant so much to him. He didn't even know who I was anymore. Mom said he got into everything. Everything—unmentionable things in the kitchen, and in the bathroom. It was constant. He lost track of time. Death knocked early on Dad's door. He was still in his fifties. Because it was Early Onset Alzheimer's, the decline was rapid. It wasn't long before he was escaping the house regularly. Luckily for Dad, everyone knew him. Neighbors and police were happy to help and bring him home to Mom. Unfortunately, we didn't have a name for what he had for a long time. The actual diagnosis came much later, too late for medication to be of assistance. "Dad was possessed like Jenny" was what we settled on as an explanation for his behavior. (Yes, to answer the next question, we tried black magic to undo the black magic his Indonesian girlfriend performed to get him like this in the first place.) Must be a curse. It was the only logical thing. After all, the doctors had given us little answers and even less hope. We turned our energies toward taking Dad to temples and seeking out Muslim bomohs, Chinese healers, Indian healers, anyone. Finally, with Debbie's help, they discovered the illness at UKM (University of Kuala Lumpur). One minute Dad was fine, the next he was demented. And then he was dead. The disease dragged on…and then it was over. I wasn't there for much of it. I had to pray about everything.

I was glad I had learned reiki while in Hong Kong in an effort to heal Dad from a distance. Every day, morning and night, I focused on my blessings and prayed for Dad's illness to turn around. I chanted a mantra, and I used a proxy, which was a pillow or a wallet at the time. It symbolized Dad. I prayed for peace. It was during one of these sessions that awareness hit about Dad's state when I was in Borneo. He grew quiet in our last year together, became less authoritative. Dad had mellowed. He was less active and didn't scold his workers so much. He appeared to be less of a supervisor, both by words and by deeds. I took that as a new facet of his complex personality. This was my new, mature dad. It wasn't. It was the disease. I could see that one day while praying.

Reiki was my small contribution. The time I spent trying to heal Dad and Jenny, and bring Mom comfort, well, it was better than doing nothing at all....

Even as someone who was removed from the everyday-ness of Alzheimer's, I felt a tidal wave of change in the home upon his death. That's when the decision to resign hit me. To make Mother adjust to this massive shift all on her own, didn't seem fair. Taking her from this environment, and allowing all this emotion from caregiving and disease to settle and adjust, to fade to white on its own, seemed like the best idea. It certainly couldn't have been the worst idea, I thought, as I helped her pack.

She was exhausted. I could see that. All she wanted to do was sleep. That's all she kept saying.

"Hong Kong has beds, too, Mom. You'll be fine."

Mother had always said to me, "When you're poor your power will come." Her aura was weak as she packed. I knew her power would come back, but I wanted to help. That was my only intention at the time.

And I wasn't very poor anymore. After only making Cs at best in high school, the University of Life had been good to me—assistant to the assistant, bookkeeping at the club, jack of all trades in Borneo, manager in charge of club promotions, building the equestrian clubs, personal assistant to the Inflatable King—these careers taught me much. And travel all over the world due to work had paid handsomely. But, I've been relying on Mother's words since I was a poor girl, since the only title I had was the rubber tapper's daughter. This was before I won the lotto for school, and long before I had lost my first dream the day I scalded my arm. I was just hers. I hoped the power from which I drew insight as an adult was this power—from my childhood. It's easy to be a king when there are servants at your feet and gold swinging from your neck. You look like a king. Everyone assumes you're a king. But to believe that a few rubber seeds in your holey pocket are diamonds, until one day they are, well, that's the strength Mom was referring to—the strength of a rubber tapper's daughter. She was the daughter of a tapper, too, so she knew what she was saying. A vacation from this reality was more about bringing her back to herself.

So, Mother was mine for a year. I was so lucky. The first thing on our agenda was to cruise the Yangzi River in China. She had seen China with Angie a couple of times, but never from the perspective of a cruise ship where the view is never ending.

The Yangtze River is the longest river in China. Its shores are rich with cultural relics. We went from Chongqing to Shanghai. Along the journey, we also got to see Jinyun Mountain, Fengdu Ghost City, Yunyang Zhangfei Temple, Jingzhou Ancient City, Red Cliff, Wuhan Yellow Crane Tower, and Yueyang Tower. We stopped at all the big cities along the way from Chongqing to Wuhan to Nanjing to Shanghai.

The Three Gorges is something everyone should see in their life-time. This is the world's largest hydro powered dam. If you don't believe in God before you see it, you will afterwards; it's majestic. It's one of the top ten scenic sights in China. It starts in Fengjie County in Chongqing City in the west, and ends at Yichang City in Hubei Province in the east. It's composed of Qutang, Wu And, and Xiling Gorges, thus the name Three Gorges. A large number of celebrities throughout history have written poems and fashioned paintings praising its charm. After nearly twenty years, the completion of the Three Gorges Dam Project was final in 2009. The structure in its totality is just shy of 4,000 square miles.

Mom read incessantly during our time on the cruise. She came to know a lot about the history of the Yangzi River's stops. She had so much to share. I remember being on the deck with Mom. The wind was always wild up there. Red mountains in the background framed Mom's face. The sun was setting. She looked like she was posing for a famous painter. She was a goddess, my very own princess. I was so blessed; I was raised by a princess. Like Cinderella, her time had finally come. She was getting a much deserved, long overdue break after all these years of taking care of us, and Dad. In that same moment, I remember wishing Dad was cruising with us, too. But then as the sun went down, the wind grew cold.

We needed to go inside the boat. The moment had passed. It was cold now.

Mom was relieved to be done paying back karma. And her worry about Dad not eating or sleeping or losing his way home was over, too. Her joy and freedom were palpable. I was so glad it was God's will I spend time with my beautiful mom. We ate on the boat, exercised in the gym, learned to write calligraphy; we sang karaoke, took cooking classes, and were simply content to be together. We smiled at each other all day long. I was consumed by happiness.

The boat would stop and we'd take smaller boats to see the sites. Mom had so much energy. She was ready to be part of the excursion team, to swim, pick stones, and do all the sightseeing they had to offer.

I think it did the trick. She was revitalized and rested. She was a new woman. She even looked younger. Like I said, she became a princess on that boat.

I took the trip back with her. As I had hoped, the house was at peace. The ghosts of caregiving had slipped out the cracks below the doors and the windows. Her home was a symbol of freedom for her again. She worked hard for that home; it was time for her to enjoy it.

Pau Chu moved in. Mom wasn't going to be alone ever again. I don't mean to imply that she was alone before, when Dad was there, but in a sense....

———————◆———————

I visited Dad before departing. His handsome picture on the granite stone was lovely, and the lawn was well manicured. Part of me was sad he was alone. That's silly, I know. It's not like his soul was pressure-sealed inside a mason jar and buried in the ground. I felt tragically small and human, and even shallow about such concerns. I shook that off and surrendered to the peace around me. Dad was not lonely. He was safe now. He suffered so much. He worked hard in life and even harder for his death. It was a real dogfight. It is said that like birth, so is there work in death. Dad certainly earned his right to die. Alzheimer's had a way of ensuring that, too. But I didn't feel that energy here, from the fight of it all. I studied the beautiful birds of paradise, and watched the breeze rustle the leaves in the frangipanis trees, and all I felt was serenity.

I thought of the natives of Borneo, and how simple it was. I thought of father back when he was of sound mind, coexisting with them. Would he have wanted to be buried like they were? Would those have been his wishes had he been able to express them? Mom, Debbie, Richard, Angie, Charles, and Jason had stayed with him, too. Did they know the man I'd come to know before his memory was taken?

Dad was not a father who brought home riches. He taught through action. His zest for hard work was what we learned from our father. He was smart and patient. That I learned as an adult, about his patience. Siblings 1, 2, 4, and 5, they went to English schools thanks to Father. We learned world history, geography, mathematics, biology and other sciences, as well as English, because of Dad's insistence. All subjects were in English. Every trade Dad had acquired throughout his life was self-taught: mechanics, logging, supervising, hunting, fishing. Dad spoke Mandarin, English, Bahasa Malaysian, Bahasa Indonesia, Tamil, and the dialects of Hainanese, Hokkien, Mandarin, and Cantonese fluently. He picked these up along his path. When he was quite young, he couldn't converse casually with his English bosses; that's when he made it his mission to learn English, and vowed that his children would know it too. Communication was everything to Dad. And because Dad was such a talented mechanic, the English management hired him to operate the movie projector in Kluang for Lambak Estate Community Hall on Tamil and Hindi movie night. He had such a deep understanding of how things operated. He was perfect for the job. Bollywood cinema for all! Who could ask for more. This was considered one of the perks for Rubber Estates 1, 2, and 3. About one hundred and fifty people would gather around late in the afternoon for one of Dad's double feature events. We'd bring carpets and mattresses in order to really settle in.

Everyone had their Tamil/Kollywood and Hindi/Bollywood favorites in the '60s through the '80s: Nagesh, Jai Shankar, MGR, Sivaji Ganesan, P Muthuraman, Padmini, and Jayalalithaa Jayaram, Raah Kumar, Meena Kumari, Ragesh, Mumtaz, Amitaba Bachchan, and Rekha. I was so in love with these movies.

When Dad left home, the estates waited all year for his return to unite everyone—Muslims, Indians, Chinese—on mattresses with snacks for four hours on Saturday, so we could laugh and cry and love with our onscreen stars. We were no longer three cultures; we were merged into one big family enjoying an evening together. Dad did that for the community thanks to his extra special talent with the projector.

I must confess, I'm still crazy about Hindi movies and all their dazzling stars like Aishwarya Rai Bachchan, Hrithik Roshan, Anupam

Kher, Madhuri Dixit, Shabana Azmi, and Kareena Kapoor. I have Dad to thank for that. Movie nights and the sweet moments together in our community house in Kluang. That's the Dad I hold in my heart forever and ever, the one who made that possible.

Please, let there be no fuss, Ah Lian. I lived in the jungle and I will be happy to die in the jungle. Sit me up straight with my legs crossed, like the Yogi. Say a prayer. Leave me with my best hunting knife, and cannas lilies. Plant them right next to me: my loyal friends, longest companions. That's what I imagined him saying. *I'll be fine just like that. Free like the morning mist.*

This was not Borneo, but it was pretty. I read the names of the strangers buried on either side of Dad. They were older than him. They had nice names. He wasn't alone.

Everything was going to be okay....

chapter twelve

People with nine as their lucky number are able to freely create an easy and relaxed atmosphere for themselves and others.

"EXCUSE ME, SIR? DO you know where my sister-in-law and I might find some good Chinese food?" I asked a fellow vendor. He was a mature gentlemen. He had helped me carry a box in earlier. He seemed like he knew his way about the furniture show. I was hoping he knew of some authentic Chinese food in San Francisco.

My sister-in-law, Wong, and I were up from LA. We had temporarily moved into a motel in Santa Monica for a couple months till we established everything. We were working to set up sister furniture stores in Pasadena, Palos Verdes, and Newport Beach; we were running the US office for Charles. It was 1998. San Francisco was our first furniture show.

Before and after my personal assistantship with the Inflatable King, if you recall, I had studied my brother's business briefly, and helped set up wholesaler clients in Hong Kong. Charles was busy with furniture production at the home base in Indonesia. Two months back, the paperwork had come in. I was cleared to go to America to run IDF, a division of my brother's Queen Anne Furniture Collection. Louis the XV, XVI, and Napoléon the Third mahogany style furniture were also branches of his company. His furniture and the manufacturing plant were impressive. Excellence was the name of his game. No two pieces were alike, as they were all hand carved, kiln dried, sanded, varnished, adorned with gold and silver leaves and painted individually. In spite of the heat and humidity, sawdust flying around, a strong and steady varnish smell, and noise of sawing and cutting from all the furniture making in the warehouses, it was exciting to watch the production lines and see the finished products. It was so satisfying. Everyone worked as a team from 6:00 a.m. to 3:00 p.m. every day of the week to create spectacular and inspiring furniture that was so easy to talk about. But the prices were "spectacular," too, and therein lied the challenge that would one day bring down the business in America.

"There's an amazing Chinese restaurant just three blocks down the hill," the gentleman responded. "Go through the stoplight. It'll be on the southwest corner. You'll know it when you see it. If you're willing to wait, I would be happy to escort you ladies. My treat."

"Oh, no. No, thank you. We'll be fine."

"Well, it doesn't get any better than that. It's the best in San Francisco, maybe all of California. Southwest corner, just after the light. Enjoy."

"Thank you so much. Have a good evening."

Wong and I were so happy to get off our feet and rest our aching backs, we would've eaten anything by the time we reached the restaurant. And we did…eat anything but Chinese. This was a French-Vietnamese restaurant. This type of cuisine was the result of the French occupying Vietnam—duck's liver with French bread, grilled rabbit, onion soup, and mixed salad.

Wong and I gave each other a look as we ate in silence.

Finally, I said, "I guess that's what I get for asking a White guy where to get authentic Chinese."

We both chuckled.

"Yes, but if someone asked you where to grab an American burger, you wouldn't direct them to the nearest Pizza Hut."

"Come on, Wong, it's not that bad." I reiterated in Chinese. She didn't know much English.

"It's the difference between ginger garlic stem catfish and grilled codfish with black pepper onion."

The cooking and taste of the two cuisines were vastly different.

"It is funny, though," I added.

"It is funny," she agreed.

We continued to giggle as we ate roasted duck, lobster bisque soup and French bread, which we dipped into the broth of the escargot.

———◆———

Setting up the surrounding LA stores, we worked twelve or more hours a day, seven days a week. Between that and attempting to teach Wong both English and how to drive in the states, I had little time left to myself. Of course, I still had my goals:

Detaching was part of the plan. Mastering the skill of detaching was developing nicely in America. I had no friends and no time to date. Sometimes the Universe cuts a person a break like that.

To give and to share with others was another main goal. I had to work on that. I was generous, or am generous, but at that time—my first year in America—the drive to succeed dominated over generosity. Naturally, I had a business to run, and it wasn't even my business, and so prosperity and success were always on my mind.

Marathons: how I longed for the freedom of running. I wanted to fit one or two of those in. But hauling all the furniture, plus the intense working hours, was getting to me. My back was feeling strained more and more regularly. I put that goal on the back burner, figuring, I'd search for a marathon and train "next year."

I remained open to the future as I led a life of all work and no play. I had heard rumors that the USA was where dreams came true. Big success stories happened here. Both my girlfriends from the properties division were here, Sharon and Wati. They were doing well. I hadn't seen them though. There was no time for playing around in the furniture business. The shows (that took place all over the country) went on twice a year—San Francisco, Las Vegas, the Los Angeles Convention, Long Beach, High Point, and Atlanta. Packing and unpacking massive amounts of stock and putting it on display was our new way of life. This was the opposite of backpacking, where you have one bag with all those trick pockets to fit everything you needed. Try strapping a hand-carved mahogany coffee table with matching end tables onto your back. The work was endless. We'd make our way around the country, and as soon as there was a moment to breathe, it would start all over again midseason. That's what landed Wong and I back in San Francisco before we knew it.

One Year Later

"Hi there. Excuse me? Do you have a hammer I could borrow? I seemed to have misplaced mine." I asked the gentlemen from last year—the one who didn't know Chinese from a cheeseburger.

"Here you are, miss." The gentlemen smiled as he handed me a hammer. "You can keep that if you like. I have another. How are you, by the way? It's good to see you."

"I'm fine, thank you. I'll be right back!" I said, motioning with the hammer.

One Hour Later

"Here you go. Thank you." I handed the gentlemen his hammer.

"Think nothing of it," he said.

Then I stood there biting my lip, until I couldn't help myself. "You know, last year you directed my sister-in-law, Wong, and me to an authentic Chinese restaurant."

"Yes, I do recall."

"Well, it wasn't Chinese. It was French-Vietnamese. It was very good. Thank you very much, but…. Well, I thought I'd mention it, just so you know."

Through a prominent grin, this gentleman replied, "I think you must have went to the authentic French-Vietnamese restaurant across the street from the authentic Chinese restaurant."

"Oh." I wasn't expecting that…. "We didn't see another restaurant."

"The real authentic restaurants, well, you know how they are about advertising. They're not very flashy."

"No, they are not." *Look who's the fool now, Rina.*

"Why don't you let me make it up to you. I'll take you and Wong to dinner there tonight, after the show."

"Oh, that won't be necessary. Clearly it was my mistake."

"I'm terrible at giving directions. Let me make it up to you. It would be my pleasure. I'm Marshall."

"Thank you, Marshall. That would be very kind. I'm Rina. We will meet you here at seven for…authentic Chinese."

Marshall was right about the restaurant. It was amazing. Everything was authentic, not just the food—the motifs, spoons, rice bowls and plates, chopsticks. The wooden chairs were painted

164

intricately; they were low to the ground, like the tables (of course). I nearly went into the kitchen to double check that Grandmother wasn't back there cooking. The food was that perfect. We had sweet and sour seafood soup, Hakka yum pork stews, stem fish, salted fish fried with bean sprouts and spinach fried with garlic. We ate our hearts out. The aromatic jasmine rice was such a treat. It was soothing to eat a home cooked meal. I felt like I was a tiny girl back in Mom's kitchen in Malaysia. We thanked Marshall for being so kind and generous. He took care of the tab for us, too.

One Year Later

"Rina. Hello. How are you, my dear?"

"Marshall. Hi. I'm good. New year, new show. Same Rina, still working." I smiled. "What's new? How are you?"

"I haven't found any authentic Chinese in Atlanta, but I'd sure love to take you to dinner when we get back to LA."

"That's so sweet, but I don't have time. I'm sorry. I work every day."

"My restaurant has excellent seafood. I'd love to have you in, Rina."

"I'm really too busy. I so appreciate your offer but, Wong and I, the company needs us both, you know."

"I'll take you both to dinner."

"That's too much, Marshall. Plus, my sister, Angie, she's in town."

Angie was in America. She had quit Cathay Pacific and was an agent now in the ceramic business. She was the link between the Hong Kong and American markets because she was bilingual.

"It would be a pleasure to have all three of you ladies at the restaurant."

"I really don't have—"

"Rina, everyone needs to eat. It's just one date."

"Well, in that case, you should know that I can't date you, Marshall. That's out of the question. I'm a working woman making my way in the world. I'm interested in making a profit, gaining knowledge, and building a savings. I'm not planning on having babies. That's not my destiny. I don't—"

"I already have babies. *They* have babies. I'm not looking for babies. Do I look like I'm looking for babies?" he asked, and then he studied me for a minute. "You know, Rina, I'll need to take you on at least one date, if I'm going to marry you."

"Marry me! That's American talk. Don't push your luck, Marshall. I'll give you one date with Wong, Angie, and me. We'll be there. Let me know when...."

One Week Later

I had lobster for the first time in my life at Marshall's restaurant in Santa Monica. It was wonderfully juicy and delicate and rich. Wong and Angie brought their appetites as well. Angie also brought her book of ceramics. Each course of the meal took place between her pitching products to Marshall. I'm sure this caught him off guard, although we couldn't tell. He ordered more ceramic pieces than I'd ever seen a single client do. Angie really hit the jackpot with this guy. Maybe he knew something I didn't about ceramics.

After that evening, Marshall wanted to know when it would be just he and I at dinner.

I knew that was coming....

I started in on the speech about my destiny again, about how I'm an independent businesswoman, detaching from worldly possessions while simultaneously becoming very successful and self-sufficient. He rebutted with the speech about how a girl's gotta eat.

I explained my hours: 8:00 a.m. to 10:00 p.m., 24/7. He said he'd be at the Palos Verdes store at 9:45 to take me to dinner after I closed up.

And so it began. Marshall drove from Woodland Hills weekly, sometimes getting stuck in traffic for hours, to take me to dinner after work on Fridays. Flowers, phone calls, hand written poems started coming in regularly, and by the dozens, too. His style was so Hollywood—chasing me like he did. This became routine for the next year or so: work, dinner with Marshall, a constant stream of fresh flowers to brighten my new American life. I was happy, but at the same time nervous, not knowing where this was going. I prayed and prayed that God would lead me to the perfect path of my life partner. My priority and goal was to establish a furniture business, and, of course, to make money. Everything else was secondary. *Why was Marshall in my life right now? What did it mean?* The man I was slowly coming to know was one of amazing patience and generosity. He had brains, too. He was a doctor, businessman, sportsman, and restaurateur. But, oh, what would Mother think. I prayed to God about her, too. Marshall was White, Jewish, older; he had children and grandchildren…and I had nothing. He had passed the Angie and Debbie test. That eased my mind a little. I just couldn't imagine Mother ever accepting this man, not the mother I knew growing up. That mother did all she could to segregate Muslims, Indians, and Chinese. That's why Jenny and I stole away to celebrate our neighbors' holidays so much.

Hari Raya, one of the biggest Muslim holidays, was one of our favorites. This Festival of Forgiveness has been a tradition for over a thousand years. People from all over return home to visit ancestors' graves and repent together.

Deepavali, also known as *Diwali*, is a festival of lights celebrated by those of Hindu faith. Jenny and I ducked out annually to join in that merriment. Deepavali is an official holiday in Malaysia as well as in some Asian countries like India, Myanmar, Mauritius, and in non-Asian countries like Guyana, Trinidad and Tobago, Suriname, and Fiji. Small clay lamps filled with oil are lit embracing the power of good over evil, and the lights are kept on all night. Homes are cleaned prior to the festival to welcome the goddess Lakshmi. Paper lanterns and *kolam* (designs on the floor made with colored rice) are strewn about. This holiday is like Christmas for Americans.

Mother moved us, for goodness sake, in an attempt to prevent us from mixing too much with our ethnic neighbors and their special holidays. She and the whole family disowned my aunt when she married an Indian man, by the name of Arumugam. They were right there locally, in Kluang. Arumugam literally means Lord of Six Faces. The name implies wisdom and all knowing capabilities to see north, south, east, west, Earth and sky simultaneously. The name is revered, and even worshipped, and it's doesn't get more Indian than that. It's been twenty-five years since they've spoken with my aunt. How was this supposed to work? My heart beat faster and faster every time I thought about it.

What I didn't know was what the future looked like. How could I, it was the future. I didn't know Marshall spoke fluent Bahasa (Indonesia and Malaysia), and would be able to communicate so effectively with Mother. I didn't know he'd take so many regular trips to Malaysia, and visit her every time. I couldn't have known that he'd turn into a son in her eyes, just because of the love he had for her, or that he'd be so generous with her and my other family members, too. All I knew back then was that this man was in love with me. He was writing me poems, and leaving me voice messages that I referred to as my musical phone calls. He was winning over my heart, day-by-day, bouquet-by-bouquet.

God please guide me to the best life you want for me. As your child, I pray to you.

December 31, 2001

There I was: Chinese-jungle-girl-turned-American-businesswoman hand in hand with my distinguished Jewish-doctor-business-mogul boyfriend. We were at a chapel in front of an ordained minister who was dressed like Elvis.

Vegas, baby.

This is just like Mom imagined, I thought, as I said my "I do's." *Just like in the fairy tales....*

————— ◆ —————

I hadn't had a Sunday off all year, and it was nearing summer. Marshall's son was home from Cornell and he was having a pool party. He invited some close neighbors, along with his children and grandchildren. He begged me to come, said he'd teach me how to make American food—barbequed everything—chicken, baby ribs, salmon (we'd stuff that, not barbeque it). I said okay.

By the time I got there it was one in the afternoon and Marshall had everything done. That was just like him. I was so tired from working seven days a week for months on end, I rolled into the hammock by the pool beside the rose garden and fell asleep. What a terrible guest I was. (And I was meeting his son, daughter, family and friends for the first time, too.)

When I woke up, he was by my side, with a ring and a request for my hand in marriage.

I couldn't help it, I asked, "What does your son think of all this?"

He said, "He thinks you're perfect for him!"

We'd laugh about that joke for the rest of our lives.

———◆———

Marshall didn't buy one or two pieces of ceramics from Angie on our first date, he bought a two containers, imported from Hong Kong. He has since confessed that he didn't have a clue what he was supposed to do with all those pieces. He sold most of them, but took quite a loss. He was just trying to make a good impression on a first date. He was a man with a strong will and a massive amount of persistency, and he wasn't going to let a little thing like two thousand pieces of ceramics get in the way of it. He also liked the idea of Angie being an agent between China and the USA. He said you never know when you might be building future relationships. Angie does outsourcing of goods for factories in China, works with Marshall to get merchandise here, and on product development for his current furniture and accessories' lines from China to the USA. As time goes by, business is expanding in spite of all the ups and downs in the furniture and accessories industries. His initial investment has paid off tenfold.

Marshall has been sincere, honest, and unequivocal since the day I met him. That day by his pool he said should my mother or family disown me, he would take care of me for the rest of my life, one hundred and ten percent guaranteed. And he assures me daily, and promises that I need not worry about my status, about old age, or retirement. I will live well and comfortable for the rest of my life.

Wow. That was impressive. Everything he said was always so…perfect. *Was that American talk?* I had to ask myself. But then I listened to instinct, which was telling me it was going to be okay. I dove, one more time, bungee jumped without a rope tied to my ankle into this relationship…and I got lucky.

I have learned from Marshall that love is blind and love is kind. Love is about focus and determination. It's about sitting in traffic for hours. Love it patient. Love understands freedom. It speaks all languages. It knows how to hold on and let go at all the right times. Love is never worried, or confused. Love doesn't mind taking the blame, even if it doesn't own it. Love is still, and peaceful, and warm, like a nap in a hammock on a summery day.

Remnants of our first date linger about. To this day, I stumble across Angie's ceramic pieces in the house. Marshall says he likes having them around as part of my dowry…. They make me smile and warm my heart. Memories. He says they remind him of how hard he had to work for the best gift of all, the gift of love in his life.

They remind me, too….

His upfront love touched my heart. I have never met anyone as transparent as Marshall, except maybe Mother.

chapter thirteen

WHEN WE WERE YOUNG, my siblings and I were not given permission to swim in the pool at the English men's house. But we did it anyway. We never felt anything like it before. We sneaked into the pool. It was so big and deep, and the water was magical. We'd pretend the heat from the sun on the pool enabled us to float without effort. It was a contest, but one that everybody won. We floated with ease, like corpses, from that hot water.

Dad worked at the estates as a mechanic back then. The English men would pop in and check on their cars, and they'd watch us. We were nobodies, just a bunch of young carefree kids running around their gardens while our parents worked at the rubber estates. We didn't care that they didn't share. We helped ourselves. Their homes were so beautiful. They had housekeepers and gardeners. We'd refuse to leave when the sun went down. Father would have to yell. He knew what we were up to. Then we'd walk home with tears in our eyes. *We share the same sky and the same ground, God. Why do they live in mansions with magical pools and we have the bungalow? Why are we lined up nine in a row to sleep on one floor, when one English man owns five rooms?* I remembered stomping my tiny foot and thinking God was unfair. I didn't know when I was three and four and five that the sky was the limit. No one had told me, and I hadn't yet found out for myself.

After dad left for Indonesia to earn extra money for us to go to English and Chinese secondary schools, and to support the family, Mom took full charge of the young ones, numbers 8, 9, and 10.

Mom was smart. She never laid her hands on us. Her teachings were through nurturing. Because we were of Chinese descent, we had to learn how to speak and write in Mandarin. That was Mom's first plan. In spite of all the other dialects, which we already spoke at home with our siblings, grandmother, and neighbors—we even spoken Tamil with our Indian neighbors—we were to learn Mandarin. But we were so good at playing games outside—hide and seek, hopscotch, jump rope with big rubber bands. We didn't have time for school. We were so young. But Mom called the shots now that Dad was gone. She was the queen of the house, and before we could blink we were enrolled in Chinese Chong Hwa School 1 in Kluang. We buckled up for six years of Chinese education. Every subject was in Mandarin, except one class, which was in English, because it was *English*.

Stroke by stroke, we learned Mandarin. For hours and hours, every day and every night we worked on family names and simple words. It became our religion, as if we didn't have enough of that around! As time went by, sure enough, we were molded into good little Chinese students. We became disciplined. It is part of our culture that we are always thinking, working, living, playing by the

174

rules, or playing "inside the box." This gets embedded at a very early age. It's not typical to practice freethinking or creativity. The culture is so rich and there's so much history to pass on, it's understandable. Plus, we were always working on writing our Mandarin inside the box. It becomes habit after a while. And this consistent practicing of Mandarin created an environment where black and white, and right and wrong were easy to see. In Asian culture it's important to be on the right side of all that, to be part of the group. Individualism was not really taught. Mostly, I think Mandarin is such a challenging language that the art of truly knowing it requires severe physical and mental discipline. There are no shortcuts. In between practicing our symbols inside boxes, we learned Chinese History, Chinese Culture, Calculations, Science, and Geography. We had a Morals and Confucius class that preached about how to live on the right path. We learned about Chinese philosophers, and *Analects of Confucius*—a system comprised of a specific moral, social, political, and quasi-religious code of ethics. And the Three Jewels of the Tao, which are compassion, moderation, and humility, became an integral part of our studies. We learned how they were part of our ancestors' way of life, too. We were all related. My culture is wonderful.

Now that I'm a grown up, I've been able to look back and really appreciate the Chinese school and all their instruction. The teachers were so nice. They were strict but loving, and they supported the caring and sharing philosophy, too. This school prepared me for Canossian Convent School. I would have won the lotto and then wouldn't have been ready, was it not for six years of extensive preliminary education. One minute I was jumping rope and skipping rocks, playing wedding in the yard, and swimming in a pool as big as the sky, and then a minute later—I won the lotto and left for the convent school as a young girl who was fluent in Mandarin Chinese and had a decent understanding of her own culture and its history. This was no accident. Even though I had a feeling that those spring onions weren't going to bring my grades up to As in secondary school (for they didn't in the Chinese school), I went there with a sense of knowing who I was. I understood the importance of family, of my ancestors. I loved my heritage. I was blessed to have parents who valued education and wanted me to have those experiences. They knew that knowledge would be my ticket to success. I was just starting to dream about the airlines. (That's how I was going to see the world, remember?) But Mom and Dad, my teachers at the Chinese school, and those at the convent school weren't preparing me to be one thing; they were getting me ready to be a flight attendant, or a bank president, a teacher, a lawyer, a long distance runner. They were getting me ready to see the world and leap tall buildings, should that opportunity arise. I felt that. Every day I went to school, even when life got dim for a spell after my arm, I felt the power of the words my teachers spoke. I felt sincerity and joy in their teachings. I knew I was blessed.

Here are some of my favorite words in Mandarin. You can see how beautiful they are—simple yet powerful. I've always been in awe of this language.

天命– Tiānmìng– Destiny

天下:天地- Tiāndì - World

刻苦- Kèkǔ– Hardworking

细致 - Xìzhì - Meticulous

谦虚- Qiānxū– Modest

彻底-Chèdǐ - Thoroughgoing

真诚- Zhēnchéng– Sincere

喜爱- Xǐ'ài - Favorite

尊敬- Zūnjìng– Respect

爱心- Àixīn - Love

良好- Yǒulǐ- Well-mannered

慷慨:大方-Dàfāng:Kāngkǎi – Generous

自爱- Self-respect

天下无难事，只怕有心人- Nothing in the world is difficult for one who sets his mind to it.

———— ◆ ————

I played the flute in the school band at the Chinese school; that's another thing they taught me, about music. We traveled around to perform for sporting events—for the opening or closing ceremony. We played when VIPs blew into town at City Hall, and on national holidays. We practiced so much. On the bus we ate lunch, napped, ate dinner. We went all over the country. I treasured the band teachers and choreographers. We were small kids, but we had a big job, and we understood the value of it. Some of my friends had very nice shoes. You knew they didn't live in bungalows, more like mansions, like the English men. But when we all played together in a performance, we looked the same. No one noticed my shoes, or my hand-me-down jacket. They watched us as a group, a single unit. God didn't feel so unfair to me anymore, not when I was playing the flute. We all rode home tired on the bus, too. Even the kids with the shiny shoes ate rice for snacks and needed their naps.

My friend, Pang's parents owned a coffee shop. She'd bring lots of food on the bus like chicken and egg bow and fried bean sprouts with noodles. Another friend, Yong, invited me over regularly for lunch. Her grandma would cook pork with mui heong salted fish, or spicy kangkung with belacan sauce. Because I lived so far away from school, I took their invitations instead of going home. It saved Mother from extra bus fares. I have always been grateful for their friendships. Each time I go home from the USA to my hometown, I make a point to meet up with those girls.

Even though we were poor, those six years at Chinese school took that feeling of wanting away. I was too busy, for starters, to think about my secondhand shoes. Education helped my self-esteem immensely. And the school had this grand church bell announcing a new day. It should have been at the top of the Notre Dame Cathedral, this magnificent bell, not at my little school. I can still hear it today: music to my ears.

I think about life back then, and the simplicity of it all…. It reminds me of life now. I wasn't searching as a small child. I was following the directions of my elders, and getting to know the world. I have found God's path for me. I follow that today. It has brought me back to my childhood school. Marshall and I make donating a priority. I volunteer when I can, speaking at events, and setting up annual budgets every year, so that everyone knows what we have to give, so they can plan, too.

It wasn't until I met Marshall that I was able to sit still, literally. Instead of my continuous searching, I found peace in meditation. I used to feed my soul through backpacking, marathons, mountain climbing, parachuting, etc. And while I do my fair share of it still, peace comes from the silence now. It took nearly fifty years of living to understand that my home and the home of the Divine have always been the same. It's inside me. Whether I am with my Buddhist mother, or my Jewish husband, or with the Headmistress at the Catholic Convent School, I am one with everyone, as they are with me, as we are all one with the Source.

It's a very free way of thinking. I don't know that it's for everyone. I just know it's for me. I'm content with that, as even in *Autobiography of a Yogi*, Paramahasna Yogananda Ji talks about the Saint of all religions. I've been able to focus on my home study thanks to that book. And I've found a beautiful temple right in my backyard—Self Realization Fellowship on Sunset Boulevard. The Lake Shrine houses a Mahatma Gandhi Ji World Peace Memorial called the Wall-less

Temple. It represents freedom through nonviolence, a magnificent symbol for India. There's a focal point in the middle of the temple—a one-thousand-year-old sarcophagus, which has some of Gandhi Ji's ashes encased in the brass and silver coffer. Flanking the sarcophagus are two statues of Guanyin, the Goddess of Mercy. *"Peace starts from within in the hearts of each of us."* Gandhi Ji said that. It was the Father of India's message to the world. Each one of us has an opportunity to make the world a better place. Everyone can make a difference. It brings me great peace to visit this temple and see the shrine to Gandhi Ji. And I like to meditate in the temple and feel the serene energy on the lake, too. I look forward to my daily meditations. I have found balance, and it anchors my soul. At last I have found my way home.

chapter fourteen

People having nine as their lucky number create easy laughter
and encourage the people around them to live colorful lives.

WHEN I FIRST BUMPED into Marshall, he gave me his business
card. It said:

Marshall Bernes
Chief Janitor

That made me wonder. I thought, this White man, who doesn't
know the difference between Chinese, French, or Vietnamese, has
the strangest job title I've ever heard of....

I promised myself I'd find out what it meant. What I found out
was Marshall had an interesting and exotic life. It started with a string
of emergency room stories, as he was a doctor before becoming an
international businessman, and it ended with surfing, flying, biking all
over the world, and a motorcycle tour from Thailand all the way to
Singapore (to name a few adventures).

I was really surprised. Indeed, this man had much to share. He was so inspiring.

One day, I asked him, "Why Chief Janitor? What's that all about?"

He said, "When you start at the bottom, you have to do everything yourself—take out the office trash, drive the truck for repairs, clean, dust, tag all the labels on the furniture during shows, get breakfast and lunch ready for the buyers before they visit the showrooms, ensure the toilet was clean, a fresh roll of toilet paper was on the holder, hand towels were plentiful, etcetera. I do it all! I'm Chief Janitor."

I found his story to be exceptionally entertaining. He was so well spoken and witty in the recant. But he was also smiling big, like he just won a prize, and I couldn't help myself, so I asked, "So...why are you Chief Janitor? Where is your assistant? I mean if you're the chief, surely someone works under you? Where is the assistant janitor you get to boss around? Or is your ego so big that being just 'Janitor' is beneath you, and you had to add the word 'Chief' to the title...?"

Well, this comment worked like an arrow to his heart. Instead of getting angry, he laughed and laughed. We knew something big was happening between us after that.

Marshall went out the following week and made up new business cards. This time they just said: *Janitor.*

August 23, 2014

It took me a year to plan and organize our thirteenth wedding anniversary celebration. We had gotten married Vegas style (December 31, 2001). It wasn't traditional. I mean, we vowed to love and honor each other; we just didn't have family and friends there to witness it. Two years later, on August 22, 2003, we managed to pull off a formal ceremony for 350 friends and family, and then a whole decade passed. Our marriage was wonderful, even stronger, and we wanted to get the gang (of 300+) back together. It was time to share our love with the world again.

———◆———

When I married Marshall *Vegas style* on December 31, 2001, we thought we'd do something more formal and festive right away for friends and family, but life got in the way. The pain in my back that started back in 1999 grew to unbearable levels. After years of acupuncture, massages, and herbal Chinese remedies, it was time for Western Medicine to step in. I could no longer take long—or short—walks. Bending forward was almost impossible. It hurt to laugh. I was exhausted all the time. Pain is a real energy thief. I would lie on my back with my legs on a chair. It hurt that much. It must have been worse for Marshall, just watching me in agony. He had had enough and sent me to UCLA Medical Center.

In January of 2002, I was diagnosed with spondylolisthesis—forward displacement of one vertebra over the one below it, generally in the lumbar area of the spine. It could have been congenital, or a fracture that had healed badly creating a defect in the pars interarticularis. In any case, it wasn't going away without surgery.

By the year 2007, I had refined the art of being a dutiful patient. Screws had been put into my back during surgery number one (in 2003), and bones were fused. Shortly thereafter, my right wrist started acting up and I underwent a second surgery later that same year for a ganglion cyst. The screws from my back surgery became inflamed and needed removal. This led to a second back surgery in 2005. In 2006, another ganglion cyst was removed from my wrist—a total of four surgeries in four years. You can imagine why everyone dubbed me "the good patient." I slowed down. I drank even more water. I prayed more. I realized that all my hard work as a single, career-minded woman paid off in many ways, but I had compromised my health. I didn't do anything specific, like run marathons when I shouldn't have (while in pain). Looking back, I simply overdid it. I overworked myself for years, focusing on acquiring financial freedom and worldly knowledge while compromising physical well-being. I didn't feel lower back pain when I was the girl in the sky, but I bet it was struggling to come out. It wasn't until I stopped searching, stopped running that my back said: *Enough. No more high hills. No more 26.2 miles. No more heavy lifting. You weren't meant to juggle hand-carved Mahogany furniture, Rina. No more working for ten or more hours a day, seven days a week. No more, no more.*

We must listen to our bodies. Work will always be there. These were hard lessons for which I have paid dearly. And my husband—he paid, too. He spent the first five years of our marriage caring for me. The next five, I spent healing.

And then it was time—time to celebrate.

———— ◆ ————

The rolling hills of Topanga Canyon creates both a spectacular and serene atmosphere for people to gather. The land around our home has bamboo trees scattered about and mature oaks framing the property. We are very lucky to have homegrown organic vegetables like beets, kale, artichoke, park choi, cabbage, broccoli, onion, garlic and spring onion. For fruit we have sweet and sour kumquats, oranges, lemons, limes, pears, pineapples, figs, grapes, apples, berries, and there are papaya and banana trees. A Japanese garden with exotic flowers, including orchids and wonderfully scented lavender plants, makes for a wonderful place to pray, meditate, and practice yoga.

Wildlife visits daily. They come and sometimes drink water at the koi ponds—squirrels, humming birds, hawks, eagles, coyotes, deer, migration ducks, and all sorts of other birds and owls. They sing and dance and reflect, like we do. I didn't see too many the night of our celebration though. I bet they enjoyed the event from the safety of the oaks.

We hired Chinese lion dancers for the evening, with professional drummers to accompany them—to bless the house and the event with a ritualistic performance. Guests arrived from all over the world to witness the renewal of our love. In addition to family, including my mother, and friends, there were nuns and monks.

A videographer captured everyone wishing Marshall and me a long, happy life together. The compilation video that was ultimately made from our anniversary event is something we will cherish forever.

Dinner was buffet style. We had a live band and a DJ so there was a constant stream of music. We hired a crepe maker from Paris to top off the night with authentic treats. Not that either of us were Parisian...we just wanted to mix it up! And then, of course, Marshall and I toasted with champagne, blessing our guests in return, and thanking them for sharing in our celebration.

Beams of light streamed into the event to simulate moonlight once the sun had set.

And, of course, there was dancing. So much dancing.

If you'd have asked me what I'd be doing in fifty years when I was a girl running barefoot in the Malaysian jungles, I would have given you many colorful answers; but I would not have imagined this.

Every time I close my eyes, I acknowledge my surroundings and the peacefulness they bring. And I get the sense that I have been here before. Then I get into meditation mode and give thanks to the beautiful paradise that has surrounded me in this lifetime. I sincerely feel the love of Marshall; he epitomizes unconditional love. That is how I know we are soul mates. I call him my gift from the sky. He's so generous and loves my family too. My marriage has truly been a special, sacred journey. Marshall is my Shah Jahan and I am Mumtaz Mahal, and this place is my cozy Taj Mahal, this place that I call HOME.

I feel the blessings of saints from all religions. I cry with tears of happiness and joy, they roll down my face.

chapter fifteen

People with the lucky number nine are known to have a rich imagination, universal love, and be kind-hearted.

I'M NO PIONEER, THAT'S for sure. Meditation has been around for quite some time, and I'm really just a newbie, I swear, but I know about balance. I've searched in the jungles of Malaysia, the Sistine Chapel, and the Krishna Temple for it. I chased after it in marathons in Hong Kong, Europe, and Kuala Lumpur. It wasn't on that Viking boat. Machu Picchu was pretty like the postcards, but I didn't find complete balance there, or when I prayed in the temple in Sri Lanka. Prague? Berlin? They were fascinating. I'm so blessed, but life was not totally peaceful when I visited those places. The stillness was gradual. And fear didn't dash from my body in a huff one day; it was slow moving, sloth-like in its exit.

This is the one thing I knew from the moment I left my mother's arms: stepping outside the box brought me joy and freedom. And so out into the world I stepped and pounced and glided and dashed. I was like a bright pink balloon floating everywhere the wind took me.

But one day upon rising, I realized I was blown up to the max, ready to pop at any second, but I was floating and free, and couldn't stop the windy currents. That was all right for a while, except I was so filled with air you couldn't tell I was a rosy pink anymore. I looked white, like I was in shock, or super tired. Stretched to the max. I needed to release some pressure, so I could feel rosy again. So carefully, I risked it, and loosened the knot at the opening. I knew loosening the knot would start a slow leak, but I did it anyway, knowing fear and uncertainty were mixed with the air in that balloon, and I needed to rid myself of it. Traveling released some of the air, little by little all that bouncing around relieved some pressure. Every new change in my life felt right. Every time I met someone different, or went to a brand new city, or learned another language, or a new business skill, it meant freedom. I felt less pressure about the future. A little more air escaped. And then one day in America, I realized my balloon (or more literally, the woman in mirror) had a nice rosy glow again, like I did when I was a child running through the Malaysian jungle, or riding on the sedan bicycle with arms wrapped tight around Mother's middle. I was a warm shade of rose again. I was perfectly pink, and it was time to stop, and breathe, and give thanks.

Around this time, Mother phoned. "How are you, Ah Lian?"

"Wonderful, Mom, and you?"

"I am also wonderful. Are you training for any marathons?"

"No, Mom, not currently." I could hear her smile, I swear, so I asked, "What's so funny?"

She said, "Nothing is funny, Ah Lian. I am happy you finally found what you've been searching for. I am happy to hear you've stopped running."

I'm an extravert, big time. Meeting people and learning about their stories fills my soul. I hope my story inspires others, too. My education at the University of Life has been worth a hundred degrees. *Can you imagine that the campus map in my back pocket is a picture of the whole wide world? Who knew?* Maybe my mother, she might have had big dreams for me. But I was neither prettiest nor the smartest growing up. I'm the girl who made all Cs. Yet I was class monitor. I was head of the Blue House and the Red House. I was chosen for prefect. Being in a leadership position gave me confidence. Sitting in prayer with blankets to keep me warm and candles to hold my focus, that gives me peace now.

And my mother?

"Don't be greedy, work hard, stand tall..." Her words are engraved on my heart. *"It's not so much that you're thin, Ah Lian, it's that you've lost your smile."*

Her wisdom gives my bones its density.

Zen masters can pull carts with fish hooks stuck in their skin. I've seen this with my own two eyes. I've seen my mother do the same: she's tapped nearly half a million rubber trees so her kids could be free. She is my Amazonia. She is my church bell. She is the majestic Yangtze River. She is my princess. She is my Om/Aum.

My goals today?

To put this book in the hands of a girl, boy, woman, man anywhere and especially in the isolated communities deep in the jungles of our God-given world. That would be a start.

This is my gift to share because I care and I love you all. Sincerely, it is my passion to give back.

This moment only moment!

In general, people who have nine as their lucky number never, ever stop weaving their dreams....

The University of Life

My Adventures after High School 1984-Present

Father's Logging Camp, Tanjung Redep, Berau, Indonesia, 1989

Wati's Wedding, Long Beach, California, August 22, 1999
The Malaysian Charlie's Angels: Rina, Wati, and Sharon

Prime Minister Dr. M., Bosses, and Collagues
Tropicana Golf and Country Resort, Kuala Lumpar, 1992

Mom and Rina on Yangtze River Cruise, China, 1997

Boss Tony and Other Buisness Associates, Fuzhou, China, 1996

Wedding Ceremony with Family and Friends

Topanga, California, August 22, 2003

Front: Richard, Angie, Debbie, Mom, Thomas

Back: Rina, Jenny, and Yeok Poh, Topanga, California, 2003

CNY Celebrations with Teachers and Family

Diamond Jubilee Hall, Kluang, Malaysia, 2013

Front: Guests from New York

Back: Guests from Los Angeles, Topanga, California, 2014

Family Photo—Wedding Anniversary, Topanga, California,

August 23, 2014

Marshall and Rina's Wedding Anniversary

Topanga, California, August 23, 2014

A Special Note from the Author

First and foremost, I would like to give a big *thank you* to Canossian Convent School for welcoming me back for a short tour recently. It was my great honor to give an inspired speech to my fellow beloved Chinese, Muslim, and Indian students and teachers. Also, it was delightful to go to my favorite canteen and enjoy some nasi lemak, spicy enchievy with coconut rice, goreng pisang (fried bananas with teh tarik), and Chai tea. You have no idea how much I miss this in the United States.

This is the letter that has been published in the yearbooks at Canossian Convent School, Kluang, Johore:

We came from a poor family of ten. Mom was a rubber tapper and Dad was a mechanic in Lambak Estate 1 that was managed by the British. Childhood was tough, but it was simple and there were happy times, too.

Nowadays, I reflect on how tough times can mold us into strong, optimistic, spiritual adults.

During my six years at primary Mandarin School at Chong How 1 from 1972-1977, and then the six years that followed at Secondary School at Sekolah Canossian Convent from 1978-1983, I worked very hard. Everyone was so kind and friendly. It was a sociable time for me, too, with the students, teachers, and headmistress. I fondly look back on my activities in games and athletic events— volleyball, badminton, long jump, shot put, javelin, all the short and long distance running. I was proud to represent my school, county, and state—my life was so rich thanks to you.

I was given a chance to be a class monitor, prefect of the school, captain of the game house. I was an average student in terms of grades, but I shined in sports and other areas. You saw that in me.

I remembered we hardly had time to do our homework because once home, we had tons of chores, not only in the house, but outside in the farms where we lived with our grandparents in Mingkibol. I was a little younger and perhaps spared some of those chores because of that. There were pigs, turkeys, ducks, chickens, geese, and fish to feed. We had to go out, walk miles away to the fields or jungle to harvest all kinds of plants like wild yam, tapioca, and sweet potato leaves, and carry them back on our shoulders. Chopping and cooking them took time…and this was to feed both us and our animal friends. Then there was manual watering and weeding of the vegetable and fruits farms. And quarterly, in the late night, we'd have to rise to clear and empty our septic tank and carry our wastewater and feces to fertilize Grandma's vegetables and fruit plantation. There was always work to be done. Do you consider that organic?

We were very tired come nightfall. Studies were not our prime focus, getting chores done was, for that meant food would be on the table and clean clothes would be on our backs. Daily, we also had to fetch water from the well, so we had it to wash clothes, and to clean food, plates, and cups. We needed water to drink, shower, and for house cleaning also.

During school holidays we had to help Mom in the rubber estates, and in collecting firewood, and cleaning wheat in the old palm estate. We earned 0.08 per tree—RM 1.20 per day. We worked very very hard to earn our keep. There is no shortcut in life.

Right after I left school, I worked in Kuala Lumpur. I had an early working life; I was determined to achieve my goals of success, despite the fact that I was armed with just a Form Five Certificate.

I was not afraid to work hard thanks to my mom. I put in my hundred and ten percent of effort, steadily expanding my personal horizons. I learned fast and worked well with people of all levels and from all walks of life, and I cultivated an incredible network.

With my family's support, I crossed the threshold into the corporate world and traveled all over the world. By then I realized that whatever I aimed for I would surely attain. Always remember the saying: "Be careful of what you wish for, for you will surely get it." With that attitude, I acquired essential knowledge, experience, and skills, and moved up the corporate ladder. The biggest break for me was the personal assistantship to one of the biggest conglomerates based in Hong Kong, but with businesses worldwide. I traveled a great deal in that job— to the Pacific Rim, America, and Europe.

Despite my rather busy career life, I perpetuated extra-curricular traveling activities, too. I have hiked Mount Bromo in Indonesia; Mount Kota Kinabalu, Malaysia; Mount Sinai, Isreal; Monte Limbara, Sardinia. I took a Viking Cruise from Sweden to Norway and Finland. I've cruised along the Yangzi River in China; the Nile River in Egypt; Victoria Falls, Zimbabwe; Niagara Falls, Canada; Galapagos Islands, the Equator, and the Amazon River in Peru. I went scuba diving in Sipadan, both east and west of Malaysia, and in San Lucas in the Caribbean. I learned to Surf in Hawaii and in California. I took a Sand, Surf & Air Balloon ride to watch the sun set and rise in Dubai. I enjoyed formal Tea Tastings in Sri Lanka, England, and Mount Wu Yi Shan in China. I learned to ski and hit the slopes in Australia, Switzerland, Scandina-

via, Prague, and America. With a pack on my back, I traveled all over the world. I bungee jumped into Victoria Falls in Zimbabwe in Africa. Also, and this is the best, I parachuted out of a plane from 20,000 feet at Perris Lake, California.

Right now I reside in the USA. I found my best friend. He's a doctor, teacher, friend and a great husband. We're a great team, managing a successful business based in Los Angeles, and we venture to China, Vietnam, Malaysia, Canada, Mexico and Europe. We are importers and distributors of household accessories and furniture throughout the US, via major chain stores. Also, we work daily to expand our e-commerce businesses all around the world.

I have so much work to yet do, and it seems like I will always be constantly traveling and flying like a bird. My need to make change and to create jobs all over the world to make a better life for people who are just like I was increases daily. To see family, young generations receive a beautiful education, prosper and grow is really the point of everything I do, everything I live for.

Looking back, I attribute my zest for life as a Malaysian (and now as an American) from living in a multi-lingual society. My parents, family members, husband, teachers, friends and acquaintances—who I've developed relationships with throughout the various stages of my life—are from every kind of imaginable ethnic and religious background. It will always be faith that inspires the people from all walks of life to come together. I truly believe that. We will always be grateful for the chance we have to serve all the organizations and individuals we come across. There's an unspoken promise to pay back and pay forward the best way we can. This gift of freedom was given to me. It is available for everyone to enjoy, to seize.

I will be the first to admit that my journey thus far has not always been easy. Sometimes, many times, I was discouraged. But these moments were my best "teachers," for they braced me for brighter times, and have made me ever more grateful for the fruits I enjoy now. I will continue to work hard, to be content, to love, to be healthy, to be wealthy in my heart and soul, to share and care; that's my plan. Tons of good luck and a long and bright life—this is my wish to all my sisters and brothers on this planet.

From all I've gained and learned from my journey, I can now enjoy volunteering—giving back to my school and other schools, some non profit organization, temples, homes, hospitals, unfortunate kids around the world, and some that are closer to me. That has been my focus since marriage.

The biggest contributor to my success has been the school of hard knocks: experience. Support from my husband, family, relatives, and friends, and faith in self and others (including strangers I have encountered on my journey), have played an equally important role in my evolution as a purpose-driven spiritual being on this Earth. I treasure it all.

Remember, it does not matter where you come from. If you look within, and if you have a burning desire to achieve, you will reach your goals. Believe that you have the capability to be whoever you want to be. Put all your efforts forth, and you will get there. Be bold, be brave, commit to hard work, love and respect yourself, your family, and friends. Most importantly, acknowledge the Almighty Power that acts upon you and within you. This is how I discovered who I was, and found my path. Regardless if you are Zoroaster, Hindu, Sikh, Animists, Muslim, Buddhist, Jewish, or Christian, we are all the same.

We are children of God.

We are the Universe.

We are one.

We are.

I am.

In Memory of Richard Tham
We miss and love you very much.

Letter from Brother #1

Richard (sibling #4, but brother #1), worked hard to create a life for his bride and himself in Singapore. They had two daughters and a son. All three children graduated from universities. They are smart and successful. Richard ended up getting trained by Dad and worked in Indonesia for years. Dad taught him how to log in the jungle camps in Jakarta, Surabaya, Balikpapan, Borneo, and Iran Jaya Camp (all over Indonesia), and he taught him how to be a wood grater. Richard eventually went back to college online, obtaining a law degree from England. Searching for the right career was not easy, but he discovered many new talents and experienced successes along the way.

Then, when life was finally running smoothly for Richard, he was diagnosed with ALS. That's the disease that's been getting so much press from people raising money annually with The Ice Bucket Challenge. It's a terrible illness that takes away your motor functions, including speech, ultimately taking your life, often within several years of diagnosis. It is also referred to as MND, Motor Neuron Disease. The famous Stephen Hawking has had this illness for over fifty years. I have so much respect for the nonstop courage of Stephen Hawking and Jane Hawking for her book and movie, *The*

Theory of Everything, which demonstrates the devastating effects of LGD on the victim and their family. He is a shining example for the United Kingdom and all the world of the power of faith, love, and positive thinking. He has outlived his terminal diagnosis by five decades. I had hoped for the same kind of "against all odds" miracle for Richard.

Finally we reconnected. We all cried at the reunion. After that, Richard and I communicated through email.

Subject: Re: Magnificence Of Yoga, Meditation, and Prayers in Empowering Lives and Enriching Thoughts
Date: Wed, 29 Oct 2014 08:17:22 +0000

Dearest Rina,

I have to thank you so much for the informative and detailed explanation of your spiritual cultivation by taking refuge with Guru Paramahansa Yogananda (GPY).

First of all, my homage to GPY and congratulations to you in your spiritual findings and progress. In replying to your email from long ago, I'd like to share my viewpoint regarding my illness. You recently posted a family photo that brought me back to the week after Dad departed. There were three of us at a corner house in Lucky Garden with a lady, a medium where we later called upon the resurrection of Dad and Grandma's presence.

When Dad appeared, a moment of truth surfaced.

Every word with Dad has been vividly documented in my mind. It intuited me to think there is life after death. Death is just the migration of the soul from the existing physical body.

I've considered Dad's suffering and Jenny's bipolar illness. There is something in common with Dad and Jen's case, in that they both tended to involuntarily "give away" what they had. Dad sent money home, even when he was low. Jenny gives hers all away, too. Their souls are doing some form of "pay back" involuntarily against their physical bodies and minds. My misconducts, comparatively, could have been far worse. The commonality between Dad, Jen, and me is we have not had enough spiritual progress, which I will explain.

I strongly believe that the underlying truth behind a sickness is related to karma, which is not only from our own past, but associated to our forefathers who are also genetically connected to us in a special way. This demonstrates the supremacy of the Almighty in his doctrine of reincarnation and the art of retribution. Sorry, I am not trying to be rude to Dad or Jen, but I am trying to define karma. I assure you being sick makes me a stronger person, instead of being bogged down by virtue of reasoning and understanding.

I totally agree with you, Rina—that from inside out one can always practice meditation and prayers in trying to subjugate or mitigate a demonic interference, ill karma, or karmic hindrance.

The Tibetans have been practicing meditation and prayers to heal themselves from the inside out for thousands of years. What I'm trying to say is this may be new to us Asians and can be puzzling to understand.

I've been a disciple of Living Buddha Lian Sheng for years now, and I have also been practicing meditation and prayers. It is a combination of Taoism, Sutrayana, and Tantric Dharma where we pay respect and homage not only to the thirty-six trillion Buddhas, but all living beings in the six realms of Samsara and the Holy ones in the universe before we begin our meditation. This forsakes discrimination against anyone and any faith.

The beauty of medical problems like mine is there's a great chance of passing from "the union of the lungs' nerves collectively going on strike" (paralyzing the breathing). In spiritual terms this is a good sign.

So dearest all and Rina, thanks for sharing your spiritual progression with me as I have shared mine with you. There's a significant change in our Tham family currently. We all have some kind of belief in prayers. It's a blessing, and only possible through God—that we attain spiritual progress with our human bodies and minds versus a soul with a body facing the sky.

If tomorrow does not come for me, have no fear. Our Tham family history would have been written differently if Dad left us the very moment when he met with a head accident back in Kalimantan, Indonesia, or if this sickness befell me fifteen or twenty years ago. Now that Mom is well taken care of by Pau Chu and by all, and my kids are grown up, I will go in peace. I am so glad that all the siblings are hand in hand in good times and bad. What more shall I ask for? There is no point in fighting against predestination.

So, dearest Rina, if you can, try to find me through a medium where I shall try to remember what I wrote today. Hopefully, I am not taken away to prison on the other side…. Sorry to be longwinded. And, dearest Rina, having shared with you how I look at things now and in my present scenario, I leave this to your assessment and evaluation if I should be eligible to take refuge with GPY.

Take care and my warmest regards to all loved ones,
Brother Richard

With Marshall's blessing, I planned a trip to make peace with Richard on December 13, 2014. I went with a heavy heart and an open mind. After nine days of sharing and caring with Richard in the UKM hospital, I had to fly home to the USA. I gave him a red envelope filled with some money as a memento, a reminder of family. Blood is thicker than water, and we will never give up on each other. The token was for good health and good luck, too. I bid him so long as we were not sure when we would see each other again.

January 23, 2015

With family present, Richard passed in the hospital. I prayed that he would enjoy the journey, and say hi to Dad and Grandma who love him dearly, and that his meeting with God would be more joyous than he ever imagined. I paid extra attention to my deep breathing, as that's what ultimately takes the life of a person with ALS: respiratory failure. I was thankful for the ability to breathe.

With tears rolling down my face, I walked onto the balcony. A seagull swooped into my line of vision, and circled overhead. It was so free, like Richard now. He is well and alive in the spiritual world, and we will communicate via a medium for sure. I felt that as I watched the bird soar above me.

I remembered Richard told me in his October email to look him up after he goes to heaven: *"So dearest Rina, if you can, try to find me through a medium where I shall try to remember what I wrote today. Hopefully, I am not taken away to prison on the other side...."*

The day will come...I'll keep you posted.

Tham's Family Tree

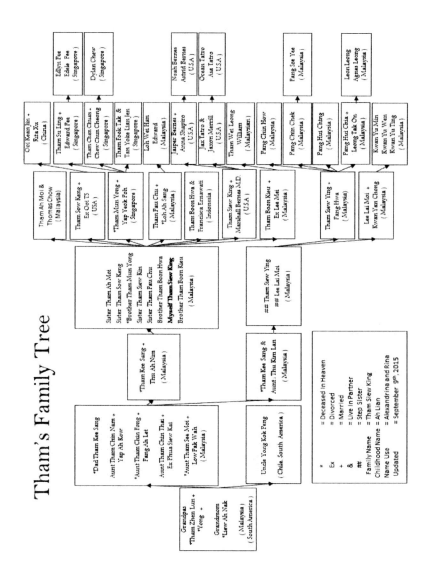

Oei Kean Jin +
Rita Xu
(China)

Edlyn Fee
Edsie Fee
(Singapore)

Tham Su Ing +
Edward Fee
(Singapore)

Tham An Moi &
Thomas Chow
(Malaysia)

Dylan Chew
(Singapore)

Tham Chen Chuan +
Chew Chun Cheong
(Singapore)

Tham Sow Keng +
Ex Ooi TS
(USA)

Tham Fook Tak &
Tan Yoke Lian Jen
(Singapore)

*Tham Mun Yong +
Yap Yeok Foh
(Singapore)

Noah Barnes
Astrid Barnes
(USA)

Loh Wei Han
Edward
(Malaysia)

Tham Fau Chu +
*Loh Ah Sang
(Malaysia)

Jasper Barnes +
Aruna Shapiro
(USA)

Ocean Tatro
Aia Tatro
(USA)

Jax Tatro &
Jaxon Merrill
(USA)

Tham Boon Hwa &
Francisca Ernawati
(Indonesia)

Tham Wei Leong
William
(Malaysia)

Tham Siew King +
Marshall Barnes MD.
(USA)

Fang Sze Yee
(Malaysia)

Fang Chun Haw
(Malaysia)

Tham Boon Kau +
Ex Lee Mei
(Malaysia)

Fang Chin Chek
(Malaysia)

Leon Leong
Agnes Leong
(Malaysia)

Fang Hui Chng
(Malaysia)

Tham Siew Ying +
Fang Hwa
(Malaysia)

Fang Hui Chua +
Leong Tak On
(Malaysia)

Kwan Yu Min
Kwan Yu Wen
Kwan Yu Ting
(Malaysia)

Lee Lai Moi +
Kwan Yan Cheong
(Malaysia)

Sister Tham Ah Moi
Sister Tham Sow Keng
*Brother Tham Mun Yong
Sister Tham Siew Kin
Sister Tham Fau Chu
Brother Tham Boon Hwa
Myself Tham Siew King
Brother Tham Boon Kau
(Malaysia)

Tham Siew Ying
Lee Lai Moi
(Malaysia)

Tham Kee Sang +
Thu Ah Nam
(Malaysia)

Tham Kee Sang &
Aunt . Thu Kun Lun
(Malaysia)

*Dad Tham Kee Sang

Aunt Tham Chin Nam +
Yap Ah Kow

*Aunt Tham Chin Fong +
Fang Ah Lek

Aunt Tham Chin Thai +
Ex Phua Siew Kai

*Aunt Tham See Moi +
Low Pak Wah
(Malaysia)

Uncle Yong Kok Feng
(Chile , South America)

Grandpa:
Tham Zhen Lun +
*Yong +
Grandmom
*Liew Ah Nak
(Malaysia)
(South America)

*   = Deceased in Heaven
Ex   = Divorced
+   = Married
&   = Live in Partner
= Step Sister
Family Name = Tham Siew King
Childhood Name = Ah Lian
Name Use   = Alexandrina and Rina
Updated   = September 9th, 2015

*For more information on the Tham Family Tree visit:

http://luckynumber9-rinatham.blogspot.com

Praise and thanks to God for Rina's innovative and creative way of sharing her experiences. *"If you live with your heart open, fear becomes an adventure…."* Caring and sharing is our way of life—what our Canossian schools have imparted to our students. Her courage to pursue her dreams is an inspiration to us all. God bless Rina and *Lucky Number 9*.

Sr Mary Tey
Canosssian Educational Coordinator
Province of Mater Dei, Malaysia

—A beautiful, down to earth story of one's journey. Living proof that the right attitude and willingness to grow spiritually pays back in many wonderful ways. Rina's commitment and dedication to life shows us that believing is achieving.

Szymon Wojcik
Yoga with Szymon, Santa Monica, California

Lucky Number 9 is so captivating and inspiring; I was hooked by the first chapter…. I admire Tham's ability to overcome the obstacles life presents at such a young age. She's an inspiration and model for our young people today, giving hope and courage.

Sr Christie Ho
Mother Provincial of the Canossian Sisters, Malaysia

Rina Tham's humble childhood, willingness to share, steely determination to excel, and ever ready ability to overcome adversity should be an inspiration to children as well as adults. I hope more people will read this book and understand that everyone is born a winner.

Mr. Cheng Meng Eng
Teacher of Sekolah Menengah,
Canossian Convent, Kluang, Malaysia

Rina's personal story of growing up in the multi-cultural small town of Kluang, Malaysia is candid and heart-warming. *Lucky Number 9* is filled with adventure and challenge, new experiences, love, endurance, and most of all—gratitude. This book will be an inspiration to all who encounter it.

Sr Esther Thomazios
Miriam Convent, Kluang, Malaysia

Lucky Number 9 is a riveting read. Having embraced openness and diversity, and having conquered her fears, Tham discovered the peace in herself that had been so elusive. In the process, she enriched her life and the lives of those around her. Her arduous journey to triumph is testament to her perseverance and resilience which was the result of a difficult childhood that was nurtured by her caring alma mater. Tham's journey, and eventual triumph is truly worthy of emulation.

Lew Mui Lian
Principal,
SMK Canossian Convent, Kluang, Malaysia

Reading *Lucky Number 9* will bring you back to center. You will ask yourself: *Who am I? What I have done so far? Can I do better?* Every child and adult must read and pass this book to those they love, just like the Olympic torch. Care and share the faith, love, and wisdom on the pages of this memoir.

Mr. Loganathan A/L Ponnambalam
Retiree Teacher, Headmaster and Volley Ball coach
Sekolah Menengah Connasian Convent, Kluang, Malaysia.